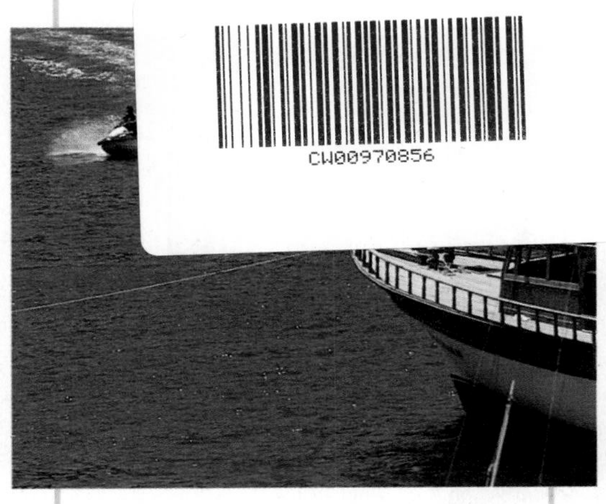

Turkey
South Coast

by Melissa Shales

Melissa Shales is a freelance writer and editor who has been travelling since the age of four and writing about travel since the age of 22. She is the author of over 20 travel guides, including several for the AA (to Kenya, South Africa, Delhi and Rajasthan, and France) and amongst various editing jobs was Series Advisor on the AA/Thomas Cook Traveller Guides and editor of *Traveller* magazine.

Above: *Watersports off Kemer beach*

AA Publishing

Boat trips are a good way of seeing the cliff-top citadel of Alanya

Find out more about AA Publishing and the wide range of services the AA provides by visiting our website at www.theAA.com/bookshop

Written and updated by Melissa Shales

First published 1999.
Reprinted Nov 1999, May, Sept 2001, Aug 2002.
Second edition 2003.
Reprinted Jan, May, Aug and Dec 2004
This edition 2006. Information verified and updated.

Published by AA Publishing, a trading name of Automobile Association Developments Limited, whose registered office is Fanum House, Basing View, Basingstoke, Hampshire, RG21 4EA. Registered number 1878835.

A CIP catalogue record for this book is available from the British Library.

The contents of this publication are believed correct at the time of printing. Nevertheless, the publishers cannot be held responsible for any errors or omissions or for changes in the details given in this guide or for the consequences of any reliance on the information provided by the same. This does not affect your statutory rights. Assessments of attractions, hotels, restaurants and so forth are based upon the author's own experience and, therefore, descriptions given in this guide necessarily contain an element of subjective opinion which may not reflect the publisher's opinion or dictate a reader's own experience on another occasion.

We have tried to ensure accuracy in this guide, but things do change and we would be grateful if readers would advise us of any inaccuracies they may encounter.

A02352
Atlas section and cover maps
© MAIRDUMONT/ Falk Verlag 2005

Colour separation: Keenes, Andover
Printed and bound in Italy by Printer Trento S.r.l.

Contents

About this Book

KEY TO SYMBOLS

- map reference to the map found in the What to See section (see below)
- address or location
- telephone number
- opening times
- restaurant or café on premises or nearby
- nearest bus/tram route
- nearest overground train station
- ferry crossings and boat excursions
- tourist information
- facilities for visitors with disabilities
- admission charge
- other places of interest nearby
- other practical information
- ➤ indicates the page where you will find a fuller description

This book is divided into five sections to cover the most important aspects of your visit to the area.

Viewing Southern Turkey pages 5–14
An introduction to the area by the author.
Southern Turkey's Features
Essence of Southern Turkey
The Shaping of Southern Turkey
Peace and Quiet
Southern Turkey's Famous

Top Ten pages 15–26
The author's choice of the Top Ten places to see in the area, in alphabetical order, each with practical information.

What to See pages 27–92
Three sections covering the main areas of Turkey's south coast, each with its own brief introduction and an alphabetical listing of the main attractions.
Practical information
Snippets of 'Did You Know...' information
Two suggested walks
Four suggested drives/cruises
Two features

Where To... pages 93–116
Detailed listings of the best places to eat, stay, shop, take the children and be entertained.

Practical Matters pages 117–24
A highly visual section containing essential travel information.

Maps
All map references are to the individual map found in the What to See section of this guide.
For example, Olympos and the Chimaera have the reference 28B1—indicating the page on which the map is located and the grid square in which the sights are to be found. A list of maps that have been used in this travel guide can be found in the index.

Prices
Where appropriate, an indication of the cost of an establishment is given by **£** signs:
£££ denotes higher prices, **££** denotes average prices, while **£** denotes lower prices.

Star Ratings
Most of the places described in this book have been given a separate rating:

✪✪✪	Do not miss
✪✪	Highly recommended
✪	Worth seeing

Viewing Southern Turkey

Above: *The Kızıl Kule (Red Tower) guards Alanya harbour*
Right: *Itinerant tea-seller in Adana*

Melissa Shales' Southern Turkey

When to Go
Winter in Turkey is generally mild, but often surprisingly grey and wet; mid-summer is often extremely hot and dry, but humid, with temperatures reaching 45°C at midday. Ideally, the best time to visit the area is in April and May, when the daytime temperature is a pleasant 25°C, the evenings are still sufficiently balmy to sit outdoors and the hills are alive with spring flowers. In spite of this, the official tourist season doesn't start until mid-May. If you prefer swimming to flowers, September and early October are still warm enough for the outdoor life, but most of the crowds have gone home.

Turkey is glorious, complicated, invigorating, confusing, refreshing, sometimes annoying and always utterly fascinating, with at least three entirely separate identities. First there is tourist Turkey, a wafer-thin veneer of expensive shops, shiny new hotels, topless bathing, beer gardens and far too much development. Next is Westernized Turkey, the reality for many Turks who have grown up in the cities or along the coast, living a European lifestyle with Islam somewhere in the background and MTV to the fore. And then there is traditional Turkey. Head inland or turn the corner into the poorer backstreets and there are women in baggy trousers and scarves, and men with hubble-bubble pipes and backgammon boards. Every road has a pothole and a hairpin bend, every house is either half-built or falling down. Hospitality, friendship and family honour codes are still the fundamental planks of society.

Finally, as if modern Turkey weren't complicated enough, add around 8,000 years of history, the wonderful mountain scenery, an impossibly turquoise sea, the baking sun, shaggy black and gold goats, olive groves and almond blossom, pine trees and wild thyme.

To me, this is a dream destination, with exactly the right mix of warmth, friendship and curiosity, history and beauty, and a rather anarchic attitude towards efficiency. I was astonished by the beauty of Lycia, loved the cities of Antalya and Alanya and, to my amazement, found the eastern section of the coast, with its echoes of the *Bible* and the Crusades and its entirely Asian lifestyle, the most fascinating of all.

View from the citadel over Alanya harbour and the 13th-century Kızıl Kule (Red Tower)

Southern Turkey's Features

• Anatolia (based on a Greek word meaning 'east') is the term used to describe the vast mass of Asian Turkey, as opposed to the tiny corner in the northwest (Thrace) that is officially part of Europe. The Romans referred to Anatolia as Asia Minor.

• Turkey has a population of about 71 million—about 98 per cent are Muslim.

• The original Turks were descended from the fiercely combative nomadic Tukin people, from the same high plains of central Asia as the Mongols. Genghis Khan was half-Turkish.

• Turkish belongs to the Ural-Altaic group of languages, together with Finnish and Hungarian, Japanese, Korean and—possibly—Navaho. Throughout the world, some 200 million people speak Turkish.

• Not only did Atatürk create modern Turkey (➤ 11), but along the way he introduced the Western alphabet in place of Arabic or Ottoman scripts, dress codes were modernized and surnames adopted. He is revered today, with his portrait in every building and his statue in every town.

• Turkey's most famous folk hero is Nasreddin Hodja, a teacher and magistrate who died in 1284. He was a wise wit who coined many famous epigrams. Stories continue to be woven around him, in film, cartoon, on paper and through folk tradition.

• Turkey covers 814,578sq km (314,427sq miles), and two continents, with the Bosphorus Straits in Istanbul dividing Europe and Asia. The country is bordered by seven countries and four seas—the Mediterranean, the Aegean, the Sea of Marmara and the Black Sea—with a coastline over 8,333km (5,166 miles) long. The Mediterranean coast is 1,577km (978 miles) long.

Crescent beaches along the Mediterranean coast of Anamur

Essence of Southern Turkey

For 2,000 years, Turkey's Mediterranean coast was the hub of the known world. Over the next 1,500 years, it faded into obscurity, its startlingly beautiful coast inhabited only by goats and fishermen. Over the last 20 years, tourism has brought a revival, while a change in land ownership laws has brought open-handed foreigners eager to own a home in the sun. The attraction is a compulsive mix of guaranteed sunshine, warm, turquoise water, hospitality, good food, a wealth of history and spectacular mountainscapes. All year round, it is enchanting.

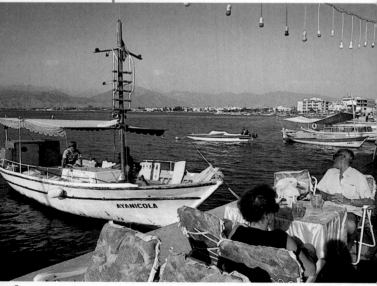

Right: *Painted dolls made from gourds are a speciality of Pamphylia*

Below: *A drink, a view and the late afternoon sun on Fethiye*

THE 10 ESSENTIALS

If you only have a short time to visit, or would like to get a really complete picture of the country, here are the essentials:

- **Drift along** past cliffs and caves, stretched out on the deck of a *gület* (traditional wooden boat), listening to the lapping of the gentle Mediterranean waves.
- **Sit at a harbour-front restaurant** eating steaming *calamari* and sun-drenched tomato salad, washed down with fresh squeezed orange juice.
- **Hike through the pine forests** and across mountains strewn with flowers, breathing in the scent of wild thyme and oregano, and then collapse with pleasant exhaustion on the walls of a ruined mountain-top city or castle.
- **Sip a glass of *çay* (tea)** as jewel-coloured carpets made from wool and silk pile around your feet and you get down to some serious haggling.
- **Stand mid-stage at Aspendos** and proclaim to the ghosts of emperors in a Roman theatre still in use after 1,850 years (➤ 18).
- **Stretch out on the sand** and spend a day working on the ultimate tan.
- **Squat on a dusty village track** talking to the local women and children and a flock of golden-fleeced sheep through mime and drawings, sharing their *börek* (➤ 50) and your chocolate.
- **Lie face-down on a marble slab** in a colonnaded steam room and let a vigorous masseur or masseuse release the kinks from your muscles and the grime from your pores in a Turkish bath.
- **Gasp at the antiquity of the area** as you visit the places where Mark Anthony met Cleopatra (➤ 90), where saints Peter, Paul and Barnabas decided to call their new church 'Christian' (➤ 80), or where the god Apollo was said to spend his winter holiday (➤ 68).
- **Party under the stars** until the early hours of the morning at a waterfront open-air disco, cooled by a brisk sea breeze.

Above: *Serious retail therapy—carpet shopping is an art form in itself*

Below: *Shrug off the cares of the day with a massage at the local* hamam *(Turkish bath)*

The Shaping of Southern Turkey

***c*6800–5400BC**
The city of Çatalhöyük (➤ 89) is established—the world's second oldest, after Jericho.

***c*1900–1400BC**
Golden era of the Hittite Empire, an advanced civilization contemporary with Babylon and ancient Egypt (➤ 20).

***c*1250BC–700BC**
Successive invaders set up new kingdoms, including the powerful Phrygian civilization, ruled by legendary kings such as Midas (in the 8th century BC).

Below: *St. Paul preaching a sermon at Ephesus*

***c*650BC**
The Phrygian Empire is destroyed by Lydians, whose most famous king was Croesus. Other Greek states developing along the coast include Lycia, Pamphylia and Cilicia.

546BC
Cyrus of Persia conquers Anatolia, which remains under Persian rule for nearly 200 years.

334–23BC
Alexander the Great sweeps across Anatolia.

4th–2nd centuries BC
Seleucids and Ptolemies compete for control of the Greek territories along the coast.

133 BC
Romans begin conquest of Anatolia, renaming it Asia Minor.

AD45–58
St. Paul the Evangelist travels and preaches widely along the coast.

313
Emperor Constantine converts to Christianity, which later becomes the official religion of the Roman Empire.

530–570
Byzantine Empire at its creative peak under Emperor Justinian.

654
Start of the Arab invasion. The coast east of Silifke becomes Arab, Islamic territory. The troubled Byzantine Empire has to fend off Arabs, Persians, Armenians and Bulgars over the next 350 years.

1071
Selçuk Turks defeat the Byzantine army. Over the next 400 years, they gradually conquer Anatolia and impose their name, language and culture on the people.

1080–1375
Part of Cilicia breaks

Kemal Atatürk—father of modern Turkey

away from the Byzantine Empire to form the independent Christian state of Armenia.

1096
The Crusades begin as Western European armies confront the advance of Islam. The Fourth Crusade is in 1204.

1098–1268
Antioch becomes a Norman, Christian principality.

1288
A minor Muslim warlord, Osman Ghazi, begins to gain power in central Anatolia. The empire he began slowly grows over the next 150 years.

1453
Constantinople is captured by Mehmet II (the Conqueror); Emperor Constantine IX dies fighting on the walls and the city becomes Istanbul (Islamboul—the City of Islam). The Byzantine Empire ends; Turkey begins 450 years of Ottoman rule.

1909
The last Ottoman Sultan, Abdul Hamid, is deposed by a group of idealistic nationalists, the 'Young Turks'.

1914
Turkey enters World War I as a German ally; Turkey wins at Gallipoli in 1915. In 1918 Turkey is carved up among the Allies.

1919–22
Turkish War of Independence.

1923
Kemal, now called Atatürk (Father of the Turks) becomes president of the new republic of Turkey. Greece and Turkey exchange minority populations. Atatürk begins reforming constitution (votes for women, equal rights, disestablishing religion and adopting the Latin alphabet). He rules as a benevolent dictator, and dies in 1938.

1939–45
Turkey remains officially neutral in World War II.

1945
President Inönü sets Turkey on the road to becoming a parliamentary democracy.

1946
Turkey becomes a charter member of the United Nations.

1952
Turkey joins NATO.

1960–2002
Military coups in 1960, 1971 and 1980 each restores power to a democratically elected leader. Coalition politics characterizes much of the 1980s and 1990s, with an Islamic-rooted party elected in November 2002. Ongoing issues include balancing Middle East and Western diplomacy.

2005
Turkey begins talks on EU entry and reforms currency.

Peace and Quiet

Flowers provide a blaze of colour throughout the spring and summer

The vivid colour of the copper-saturated sea gives the Turquoise Coast its name

In spite of extensive development, there are still huge areas of the coast empty of everything but flowers. Of course, the easiest way to get some real peace and quiet is simply to travel out of season (between October and April), when you are quite likely to be the only guest at the hotel, the only tourist at the archaeological sight, and the only shivering soul on the beach.

Deserted Beaches

To find a deserted beach in the more popular areas requires some ingenuity and the climbing skills of a mountain goat, as they tend to be tiny coves tucked into the base of a cliff. If you are content to stay in a basic *pansiyon* (➤ 102), head east of Alanya, where the cliffs protect several small settlements with magnificent beaches as yet untouched by commerce. Beyond Mersin, the water is likely to be heavily polluted.

Sail Away

Sailing holidays on traditional wooden sailing boats (*gulets*) are what the Mediterranean is all aobut. Most go under diesel power now but there are many options from chartering and crewing yourself to a full staff and accomplished chef. Whatever luxury level suits you, the 'Blue Voyage' is the way to see the sparkling bays, tiny deserted islands, sea caves and hidden coves that are otherwise inaccessible.

Green Lungs

All the major cities have parks. You can walk, drink tea or watch others doing the same. Everyone comes for the shade in summer or a small pre-prandial promenade. Karaoğlanoğlu Park in Antalya is particularly nice and overlooks the sea.

Trekking/Walking

Walking along the Lycian Way is peaceful and blissfully natural. Mostly you will have just bids for company, sometimes flocks of sheep or goats and enjoy amazing views wherever you go. Shepherds and sparse settlers are friendly and will often put you up if you are going for more than a day trip, or are weary of camping.

A babbling river beloved of trout and whitewater canoeists flows through the Köprülü Kanyon

Paragliding

Kaş and Ölüdeniz are the launching pads for this tranquil and thrilling activity. Mountain updraughts whisk you off the cliff top and you float gloriously to the beach below—just you and nature. Unless you are a certified professional, you sit tandem along with an experienced glider.

National Parks (Milli Parkı)

A few miles inland, the jagged bulk of the Taurus Mountains creates a wild, spectacular barrier between the coast and the Anatolian plain. Along them, several areas, many surrounding noteworthy archaeological sites, have been designated as national parks. You can see flowers and birds, and sometimes wild life here. Seeing the flowers emerge in spring (February to March) is an unforgettable experience. Within a month, the mountains are swathed in vivid yellow gorse and broom and by April and May the area is alive with oleander and orchids, jasmine and bougainvillea. The parks include Beydağlar Olympos Milli Parkı (➤ 44), Karatepe Milli Parkı (➤ 20), Köprülü Kanyon (➤ 64) and Güllükdaği Termessos Milli Parkı (➤ 48).

The Olympus National Park provides excellent opportunities for hiking and bird-watching

Southern Turkey's Famous

Divine Celebrities
Even the gods visited this coast. Leto brought her children, Apollo and Artemis, to the Letoön (➤ 42) to escape the jealous wrath of Zeus's wife, Hera. There was a famous oracle of Apollo at Patara, and it was supposedly in Daphne (Harbiye ➤ 83) that Paris gave the fateful golden apple to Aphrodite in return for the world's most beautiful woman, Helen—thereby sparking off the Trojan Wars.

St. Paul

Paul (originally known as Saul) was born in about AD10 in Tarsus, between Mersin and Adana on the south coast. He was a Jew, Roman citizen, tent-maker, rabbi and Pharisee, who eagerly persecuted the Christians until a blinding vision on the road to Damascus converted him to Christianity. He promptly channelled all his missionary zeal into spreading Christianity to the Gentiles, keeping in touch with his fledgling churches through copious letters that answered many fundamental questions of law, ethics and doctrine. These helped to form the basic rules of the church. In about AD58, he was arrested and spent several years in prison before being executed in Rome.

St. Nicholas (Father Christmas)

Born in Patara in about AD300, Nicholas became bishop of Myra (➤ 32), and was imprisoned for his Christianity by the Roman emperor Diocletian. When Constantine converted to Christianity Nicholas was released, and served as a delegate at the crucial first Council of Nicaea in AD325. He is said to have left purses of gold as dowries for three girls who faced penury and a life of prostitution, to have brought back to life three children who had been chopped up and pickled by a butcher, and to have performed numerous other miracles and acts of kindness. As patron saint of Greece, Russia, prisoners, sailors, travellers, unmarried girls and merchants, pawnbrokers and children, he has a huge cult following throughout Europe (his feast day is 6 December), and is widely associated with Santa Claus—derived from Sinterklaas, a Dutch variant of his name.

St. Paul of Tarsus did more than any man except Jesus to promote the spread of Christianity

Famous Visitors

The great Egyptian pharaoh, Ramses II, sacked the Hittite city of Açana Höyük in 1285BC; Alexander the Great romped through in 334BC, and, in 65BC, the Roman general Pompey rampaged along the coast. Julius Caesar was the first of many Roman emperors to visit (in 47BC) and in 41BC, Mark Anthony met Cleopatra here. Of many early Christian visitors, the most important was St. Peter, who lived in Antakya between AD47 and 54.

Top Ten

Above: *The Roman theatre, Aspendos*

Right: *Turkey's cities were also art galleries*

1
Alanya: İç Kale

28C2

Castle Road, central Alanya

Daily 8–7

Soft drinks stands

From the harbour below (➤ 60)

None

Moderate

Alanya city (➤ 57–60)

Surrounded on three sides by sheer sea cliffs, there has been a fort crowning Alanya's towering castle rock for at least 2,500 years.

A massive 250m (820ft) rock promontory, its top encircled by the huge defensive walls of the İç Kale (Inner Citadel), slices flat, sprawling Alanya in two. From the battlements, you get an idea of the citadel's true size. The outer curtain reaches right back to the harbour, surrounding the whole steeply stacked old town with a 7km (4 mile) wall.

There are 150 bastions, including the Kızıl Kule (Red Tower, ➤ 59) and around 400 water cisterns. It took 12 years to build.

The town's earliest incarnation was as a Hellenistic frontier post, known to the Romans as Coracesium. The first known fort was built in the 2nd century BC by a pirate, Diodotos Tryphon, and destroyed by Pompey in 67BC. Mark Anthony later gave the town to Cleopatra. In 1221, it fell to the Selçuk Sultan Alâeddin Keykubad I, who restored the city as his winter retreat.

The vast citadel at Alanya was the crowning achievement of Selçuk Sultan Alâeddin Keykubad I

Few structures within the citadel remain intact, though there is a small Byzantine church with fading frescoes. A fenced platform marks the Hurling Rock, or local execution point. Legend says that the condemned man was given a pebble to throw: if it landed in the water, he was freed; if it hit rock, he was heaved over the edge.

There are nearly 5km (3miles) of steep hairpin bends up to the walls of the İç Kale. There is an hourly bus service, but a taxi is worth every lira; or you can walk down through the partially ruinous old town (➤ 58).

2
Antalya Müzesi

This museum holds a world-class collection of classical sculpture, prehistoric and ethnographic exhibits from Mediterranean Turkey.

28B2

Kenan Evren Bulvarı, Konyaaltı; 2km (1 mile) west of the town centre

0242 235 5688

Tue–Sun 8.30–5

Café with drinks and light snacks (£)

Dolmuş (shared taxi), taxi, tramway or bus

Few, access reasonable

Moderate

Museum shop in the main foyer, Dösem Ministry of Culture shop in the grounds

Above: *An elaborately carved sarcophagus*

Below: *A statue from the museum*

Antalya's spacious, purpose-built archaeological museum is not huge, but has a world-class collection of classical sculpture, prehistoric and ethnographic exhibits from Mediterranean Turkey. Immense care has gone into presentation, lighting and explanation. Each piece is seen at its best and can be appreciated not only for its artistry, but for its place in the long history of Mediterranean Turkey.

The tour begins with a children's room containing a detailed model village and tables where children can play under supervision while their parents wander round. A small natural history section gives way to detailed prehistoric record, with tools such as palaeolithic scrapers, hand axes and arrowheads from the Karain Mağarası (➤ 37), Bronze Age burial urns, jewellery and toys from the Elmalı area (➤ 41) and early pottery from Aspendos (➤ 18).

In the Perge Gallery, magnificent 2nd-century statues from Perge (➤ 24) introduce the classical era. Beyond are other Roman and Byzantine statues, sarcophagi and a display of amphorae and other nautical items recovered from early shipwrecks. Most interesting are the renovated Sarcophagi Hall and Gallery of the Gods. The silver collection, with items from Elmalı, should not be missed.

Finally are the collections of coins, mosaics, and the supposed reliquary of St. Nicholas (➤ 14). The final rooms deal with later Turkish lifestyle and civilization, with displays covering everything from Turkish baths to carpets, traditional dress and reconstructed rooms.

Outside, pleasant, shady gardens are filled with yet more urns, sarcophagi and statues.

3
Aspendos

This sweeping hemisphere of seats gives Aspendos fine acoustics

For the last 2,000 years, the world's greatest performers—from gladiators to Pavarotti—have graced the theatre of this ancient Pamphylian city.

28C2

49km (30 miles) east of Antalya, 5km (3 miles) off the N-400 through the village of Belkis

Theatre daily 8–7, May–end Sep; 8.30–5 Oct–end Apr. Closes at 4 during Festival (Jun–end Jul)

Drinks stands outside; restaurants on the approach road (££)

Dolmuş

None, partial access

Moderate

Antalya (➤ 17 and 53–6), Perge (➤ 24–5), Kurşunlu Şelâlesi (➤ 67), Side (➤ 68), Sillyon (➤ 69)

Souvenir stands outside; shops on the approach road. Festivals of folk music and dance, opera, ballet and film held in the theatre (➤ 116)

Aspendos proudly boasts what is probably the world's finest surviving Roman theatre. It was designed by an architect named Xeno, son of Theodoro, during the reign of Emperor Marcus Aurelius (AD161–80). The huge, semi-circular auditorium has seating for 12–15,000, with 40 rows of marble seats divided by 10 staircases in the lower section and 21 above. At the top is a vaulted gallery where women and the general public sat. The massive acoustic stage wall was originally richly decorated, faced in marble with 40 free-standing columns and niches for statues, many of which are now in Antalya's Archaeological Museum (➤ 17). It had an ornamental wooden sound board at the top and a wooden stage about 1.5m (5ft) above ground level, projecting out 7m (23ft). Several sets of doors on the stage were for the actors and the small doors at orchestra level led to chambers for wild animals.

Aspendos was a prosperous city, probably founded in the 12th century BC, and specializing in luxury goods such as gold- and silver-embroidered *kilims* (carpets) and wine. Alexander the Great marched into the city in 333BC, but after his death it fell into the hands of the Kingdom of Pergamum. The theatre rightly grabs the glory, but there are other remains. On the left, as you approach the theatre, are a 3rd-century AD bath house and gymnasium. On the hill behind it stand the agora (marketplace), a fountain, and an 880m (2,887ft) section of aqueduct, a marvel of hydraulic engineering dating to about AD100. North of the theatre are the Roman stadium and Hellenistic necropolis. Look also for the elegant 13th-century Seljuk stone bridge spanning the Köprüçay (ancient Eurymedon River).

4
Antakya Archaeological Museum

Antakya's museum is a rainbow of magnificent mosaics, most of them rescued from Roman villas at nearby Daphne (Harbiye).

The museum begins with a small collection of costumes and jewellery, but this is merely an overture. The four main galleries containing a breathtaking array of some 50 huge, beautifully preserved mosaics. Together they make up one of the finest collections of mosaics in the world—enough to make the long, cross-country journey to Antakya worthwhile.

The earliest known mosaics date back to 4th-millennium BC Mesopotamia, but the technique only really became widespread in the 1st century AD. Most of those on show here belong to the 2nd–4th centuries AD, when they were used to decorate floors and, less commonly, walls. By this stage, the minute chips of marble and granite had been joined by semi-precious stones, glass and glazed ceramics to create a quite extraordinarily subtle range of colours. Some of the mosaics are intricate abstract patterns; most depict classical myths and legends, the gods, the seasons, the surrounding wildlife and feasts, with a realism and depth worthy of a painting. In particular, look out for *The Four Seasons* (Gallery 1); *The Buffet Mosaic* (Gallery 2); *The Negro Fisherman* and a constipated baby Hercules in *Hercules Strangling Serpents* (Gallery 3).

The space between them is used for sculptures. Gallery 5 holds various Assyrian and Hittite statues and inscriptions from Carchemish. The last two rooms contain coins, pottery, glass, jewellery and other small artefacts. These in turn lead to an open colonnade and small garden with a few more mosaics, several sculptures, sarcophagi and inscribed stelae.

29F1

Gündüz Caddesi 1, Antakya

0326 214 6168

Daily 8.30–12, 1.30–6

Café in summer only; old town restaurants within easy walking distance (££)

Dolmuş

None, but access good

Moderate

Antakya (➤ 80–2), Harbiye (➤ 83), Çevlik (➤ 83), St. Simeon's Monastery (➤ 90)

Roman residences at Daphne were decorated with superb mosaics, now in Antakya Museum

5
Karatepe

29F2

70km (43 miles) northeast of Adana; turn off the N-400 at Osmaniye. Own transport essential

May–end Sep daily 8.30–12.30, 2–5.30; Oct–end Apr 8–12, 1–3.30. Guided tours only

Snack stand outside the gate (£); picnic area on the hill overlooking the lake outside the sight

None

Inexpensive (car park fee)

Misis (➤ 85), Topprakale (➤ 91), Yılankalesi (➤ 92)

A last surviving remnant of the powerful Hittite civilization, Karatepe's story-board carvings still guard the entrances to a long-vanished citadel.

Known to the Hittites as Aslantaş ('Lion's Stone'), Karatepe stands on a rock outcrop surrounded on three sides by the huge Ceyhan reservoir. The wooded site alone is wonderful, but the few Hittite remains, carefully preserved *in situ* in an open-air museum, are something very special indeed.

The formidably walled frontier castle and summer palace was built during the final throes of the Hittite Empire, in the 8th century BC, by a local ruler named Azatiwatas. It was abandoned after being sacked and burned by Assyrian invaders in the mid-7th century BC.

The tour follows a 1km (half a mile) circular path along part of the heavily rebuilt castle walls and through the woods to visit the two main gates, both flamboyantly decorated with sculptures. The inner walls are lined with carved relief panels, or orthostats, and entertaining Hittite hieroglyphics with almost cartoon-like drawings. The reality, of course, is far more serious: the first inscription in the upper group boastfully records the building of the city, and the peace and prosperity of the region, and threatens with the wrath of the gods anyone who dares disturb the gate. (Ironically, the gate survived but the castle and kingdom did not.) Much of it is thoughtfully also written in Phoenician, providing archaeologists with one of the keys to deciphering the language in 1915.

The relief sculptures cover a wide range of subjects, including gods, happy feasts, vicious battle scenes, bear-baiting, a tender portrait of a woman suckling her child, splendidly snarling lions and sphinx gates. The second (lower) group has been more heavily restored, but both are in good condition.

Hittite relief sculptures provide a vivid record of daily life and great events 1,200 years BC

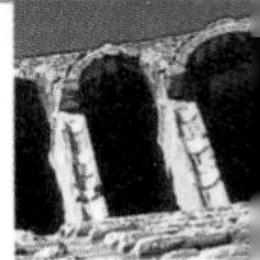

6
Kaş

One of the most popular resorts along the coast, in spite of development Kaş has kept its quaint charm, protected, in part, by its lack of beaches.

Many Greek cottages in Kaş have been converted into shops or restaurants

Kaş is one of the livelier resorts along the coast. It has no sandy beaches, but this has not prevented it from being a seasonal tourist town. Residential development continues at a fast rate and many nationalities live here as ex-pats.

Early communities in this ancient port of Antiphellos, the port for Phellos (➤ 45), made their living exporting timber and cork oaks. Latterly they engaged in agriculture, market gardening and fishing. When tourism looked like a properous alternative in the late 1970s, many people from the surrounding villages and hamlets moved into town. Today there are still only one or two holiday villages, but small hotels and tidy *pansiyons* are more easily found. The nearest sandy beach, at Kaputaş, 14km (9 miles) west, is only 150m (492ft) long and at the bottom of a steep cliff.

The town's most prominent feature is a Hellenistic theatre from the 1st century BC, close the town centre. There is a Doric tomb with a frieze of dancing girls on the hill 100m (110yds) uphill from the New Mosque (Yeni Camii), and the town's trademark is a Lycian sarcophagus dating from the 5th century BC, which stands at the top of Urzun Çarşi, the main shopping street. The eastern cliff-face also has house tombs that are illuminated at night.

In summer, boats leave from the harbour for daily tours to Kekova (➤ 38) and Simena, and also the Greek island of Meis (Kastellorizo). Kaş is a good base for trekking and dipping into the 350-km (217-mile) Lycian Way Walk, as well as for watersports like diving and sea-kayaking. On any summer day, tandem paragliders enjoy the mountain updrafts, then glide to a soundless landing on the harbour.

28B1

120km (74 miles) southeast of Fethiye; 188km (117 miles) southwest of Antalya, on the N-400

Choice of restaurants (£–££)

Dolmuş; bus from Antalya and Fethiye

From the harbour and local travel agents

Cumhuriyet Meydanı 5
☎ 0242 836 1238

None

Demre (➤ 31–2), Kalkan (➤ 37), Kekova (➤ 38), Letoön (➤ 42), Phellos (➤ 45), Pınara (➤ 46), Saklıkent and Sidyma (➤ 47), Tlos and Xanthos (➤ 49)

Kaş–Lycian Festival is held each September

7
Mamure Kalesi (Anamur Castle)

29D1

5km (3 miles) east of Anamur town on the N-400

Daily 9–5.30

Several small restaurants (£)

Dolmuş from Anamur to entrance

None

Inexpensive; a local guide is worthwhile

Anamur (➤ 78)

Mamure Kalesi, its feet washed by the waves, is one of Europe's most romantic castles

Staring broodingly out to sea, with waves crashing around the walls, this is a castle to gladden the heart of any medieval knight.

Mamure Kalesi is probably the finest of the many castles dotting the Cilician landscape. There has been a fortress here since the 3rd century AD, and by the 10th century, the first version of the present castle was in place, a formidable stronghold of notorious pirates.

From the late 11th century, it was owned by the kings of Armenia, but in 1226 the coast was conquered by the great Selçuk builder, Sultan Alâeddin Keykubad I, who virtually razed and rebuilt it. Between 1300 and 1308, Karamanoğlu ruler Mahmut Bey took control. The following century, it became a last foothold on the mainland for the crusading Lusignan kings of Cyprus, who had absorbed the title, if not the lands, of the King of Armenia. Finally, in the late 15th century, it fell into Ottoman hands and remained in use until 1921.

Today, once again restored and open to the public, it is a powerful and imposing place, with massive curtain walls sheltering two enormous courtyards. There is a small, heavily restored mosque in the centre, but the real treat is to explore the dark living rooms built into the thickness of the walls (take a torch), and to scramble along the curving battlements between the 36 bastions.

Anamur stands on the southernmost point of ancient Anatolia. It is said that on a clear day from the walls you can see Cyprus, which is situated some 70km (43miles) offshore. Even on hazier days, the view along the seaward wall to the waves pounding and crashing on the rocks beneath is magnificent.

8
Patara

Once the most important port in the Lycian League, Patara is better known as one of the most spectacular stretches of white sand beach.

Patara's white-gold sands have been voted amongst the world's best beaches

According to legend, Apollo spent his winters in Patara, which was home to a famous oracle (said to rival that in Delphi), an important trading centre, and one of the most powerful cities of the Lycian Federation betwen 200 and 100BC. In 42BC, Brutus and Cassius arrived, looking for loot to fund their war against Mark Anthony and Octavian. They took the women hostage but released them unharmed when the men refused to submit, showing themselves to be civilized. The grateful men paid up. St. Nicholas was born here in the 4th century AD (➤ 14). The city eventually died in the Middle Ages, when the harbour silted up and became a reedy swamp.

The site, scattered through fields across a large plain, is almost entirely unexcavated. Highlights amongst the many ruins include: a triumphal arch, built in AD100 by the governor, Mettius Modestus, and used as part of an aqueduct; a theatre, with 34 rows of seats (that tend to fill with sand); two bath complexes; a temple to Athena; a huge granary built by Hadrian; a lighthouse; and numerous tombs. Recent excavations have unearthed a paved street and an interesting milestone with directions to neighbouring towns written in Greek.

A boardwalk beyond the ancient city leads to the magnificent uncrowded beach (18km/11miles), with shallow swimming. There is no natural shade, umbrellas are pricey and there are few refreshments, so go prepared.

In season (May–October) this is a breeding ground for turtles. Because of this and its historic importance, much of the coast is protected, but hotels have sprung up, including in the village of Gelemiş, 3km (2 miles) inland.

28A1

Turn off the N-400 9km (6 miles) west of Kalkan; the site is 8km (5 miles) from the turn-off, the beach access about 1km (half a mile) beyond the site

Archaeological site and beach both open May–end Sep daily, 7.30–7; Oct–end Apr daily 8.30–5. On foot both are open access (the barrier is about 2km/1 mile from the beach)

Numerous options in Gelemiş (£)

Bus to Gelemiş

None

Expensive entrance fee and car park charge, even for the beach

Kaş (➤ 21), Kalkan (➤ 37), Kekova (➤ 38), Letoön (➤ 42), Phellos (➤ 45), Pınara (➤ 46), Saklıkent and Sidyma (➤ 47), Tlos and Xanthos (➤ 49)

9
Perge

28B2

18km (11 miles) northeast of Antalya, off the N-400. Turn off the main road at Aksu; the ruins are 2km (1 mile) from the turning

Daily 9–6 (later in summer)

Café and souvenir shop near the ticket booth (£)

Dolmuş or taxi from Antalya to the entrance

None

Moderate, plus parking fee

Aspendos (➤ 18), Antalya (➤ 53–6), Kurşunlu Falls (➤ 67), Köprülü Kanyon (➤ 64), Side (➤ 68

Sadly there have been a couple of attacks on tourists here, so it is probably better to tour the site in a group.

Perge is the best excavated, most complete and easily accessible of the ancient cities along the south coast of Turkey.

Although it was known to the Hittites in about 1300BC as Parha, little else is known about Perge until 333BC, when the city surrendered without resistance to Alexander the Great, who used it as his base throughout the Pamphylian campaign. Following his death, control passed first to the Seleucids, then to Pergamum (on the Aegean coast), and in 133BC to Rome, under whose wing the city flourished. However, during the Byzantine era the river silted up, leaving the busy trading port stranded 12km (7 miles) from the sea, and Perge slowly declined. Excavation and restoration began in 1947, and many magnificent sculptures and friezes found here are now in the Antalya Archaeological Museum (Antalya Müzesi, ➤ 17).

Before reaching the main site, the access road passes a 13,000-seat theatre on the left and, to the right, a huge magnificently preserved stadium with seating for 12,000, both built in the 2nd century AD.

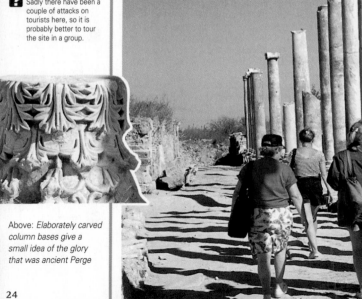

Above: *Elaborately carved column bases give a small idea of the glory that was ancient Perge*

Visitors enter the main site through a triumphal Roman gate. To the left are a nymphaeum (ornamental fountain) dedicated to the city's deity, Artemis Pergaea, and the Southern Bath House, the largest and grandest in the city, both built in the reign of Septimius Severus (AD193–211).

Directly in front are the two massive red-stone towers of the 3rd-century BC Hellenistic Gate. Between them is a horseshoe-shaped courtyard, lovingly decorated by Plancia Magna, daughter of the governor and a generous civic patron, between AD120 and 122; much of her finely carved marble lies in heaps. Bear right, along the main path, to reach the 4th-century AD *agora* (marketplace), surrounded by a colonnade with a mosaic floor and shops. The small circular temple in the centre was possibly dedicated to Hermes, the patron of merchants. From here Main Street, a 300m (984ft), marble-paved avenue, lined with columns and stepped pavements, leads through the city. Chariot marks are still visible. About halfway along, a second main road crosses, dividing the city into four. Along the way are a Byzantine basilica, a 1st-century AD *palaestra* (gymnasium) and, at the far end, another elaborate fountain. Beyond this, a path snakes up the 60m (66yds) acropolis to the site of the earliest city, of which little remains.

Inset: *The Hellenistic Gate marks the official entrance to the Greek city of Perge*

Bottom: *Perge's colonnaded* agora *would once have been alive with shops and market stalls*

10 Phaselis

28B2

18km (11 miles) south of Kemer, 3km (2 miles) off the N-400; the site is 1km (half a mile) beyond the ticket booth

May–end Oct daily 7.30–7; Nov–end Apr daily 8–5.30

Simple café (£) near the ticket booth, drinks stand in the car park; numerous restaurants in nearby Tekirova (£–£££)

Dolmuş to turning off main road (3km/2 miles)

None Moderate, plus car charge

Olympos and the Chimaera (➤ 44)

Once ships filled the three small harbours of wealthy Phaselis; today, it is in atmospheric ruins, its shady bays excellent for swimming.

Phaselis is one of the prettiest, most easily accessible and peaceful of all the ancient cities along the coast. It is an ideal place to take a towel, a picnic and a good book and spend the day sightseeing, sunbathing and swimming off one of its idyllic little sandy beaches, fringed with pines.

Legend claims Phaselis was founded by 7th-century BC colonists from Rhodes, who paid for the land with dried fish. They were ousted by the Persians, who ruled for 130 years until the arrival of the Lycians. Alexander the Great was welcomed with open arms in 334BC, and used Phaselis as his winter base.

The city prospered as a trading port, exporting timber, rose oil and perfumes, and willingly colluded with pirates. It was eventually abandoned in the 13th century AD. Its citizens enjoyed a poor reputation, however: the Greek orator Demosthenes (*c*383–22BC) went so far as to call them 'the most treacherous and unscrupulous of men'.

Sunset and a fleet of gülets *add even more romance to the ancient harbour at Phaselis*

Most of the surviving ruins belong to the Roman era. There are three small harbours: the fortified north harbour is the best preserved still used by fishing boats today; the central harbour took military and small trading vessels, while the south harbour was used by larger trading ships. The main street, lined with columns, shops, several agorae and bath houses, crosses the headland between them. At one end is an imposing gate, erected for the state visit of Emperor Hadrian in AD129. On the hill above is a small, unrestored theatre, and inland are an imposing aqueduct, a necropolis and some early Hellenistic structures.

What to See

Above: *The beautiful deep blue waters of the lagoon at Ölüdeniz*

Right: *The crescent moon and star of the Turkish flag*

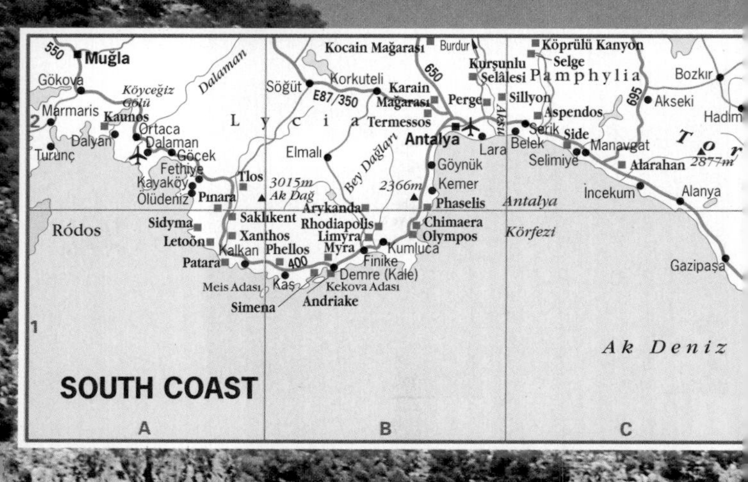
Muğla
550
Gökova
Köyceğiz Gölü
Dalaman
Marmaris
Kaunos
Ortaca
Dalyan
Dalaman
Turunç
Göcek
Fethiye
Kayaköy
Ölüdeniz
Pınara
Tlos
3015m
Ak Dağ
Lycia
Söğüt
Korkuteli
E87/350
Elmalı
Bey Dağları
2366m
Kocain Mağarası
Burdur
650
Karain Mağarası
Termessos
Perge
Antalya
Kurşunlu Selâlesi
Aksu
Lara
Göynük
Kemer
Phaselis
Köprülü Kanyon
Selge
Pamphylia
Sillyon
Aspendos
Serik
Belek
Side
Selimiye
Manavgat
Alarahan
2877m
Toros
695
Akseki
Bozkır
Hadım
İncekum
Alanya
Gazipaşa
Antalya Körfezi
Ak Deniz
Ródos
Sidyma
Letoön
Patara
Kalkan
Saklıkent
Xanthos
Phellos
400
Arykanda
Rhodiapolis
Limyra
Myra
Chimaera
Olympos
Kumluca
Finike
Demre (Kale)
Kekova Adası
Andriake
Meis Adası
Kaş
Simena
2
1
SOUTH COAST
A
B
C

Konya
Karaman
715
Göksu
Alahan
Ermenek
Mut
Cilicia
3480m
Niğde
E90/0-21
750
Mersin
Tarsus
Adana
Pompeiopolis
Uzuncaburç
Cennet ve Cehennem Deresi
Korykos ve Kız Kalesi
Narlıkuyu
Silifke
Taşucu
Gülnar
Mamure Kalesi
400
Anamur
Anamorium
Aydıncık
Ovacık
Tuzla
Seyhan
Karataş
Karatepe
Anavarza
Ceyhan
E90/0-52
Bahçe
Yılankalesi
Osmaniye
Toprakkale
İncirlik
Misis
825
Dörtyol
Yumurtalık
İskenderun Körfezi
İskenderun
E91/0-53
Kırıkhan
Reyhanlı
Antakya
420
Harbiye
Çevlik
Samandağ
E91/825
SYR
0
100
200 km
D
E
F
CAUNOS
COOP. VHF

Lycia

The most important maritime kingdom on the coast of ancient Anatolia first came to prominence in the 8th century BC, although there are mentions of the Lycian people (then known as the Lukka) 500 years earlier. They were thriving merchants and sailors, originally from Crete, whose cities were organized by King Pericles in the 4th century BC into the Lycian League. Today only their immense and elaborate rock tombs remain. Their original houses were probably made of wood.

This is the most scenically beautiful region of Turkey's Mediterranean coast, with the towering Taurus Mountains plunging straight into the sea, forming a coastline of jagged rocks and mysterious sea caves. The area was isolated and ignored, only becoming more accessible when the coast road was built in 1988. The lack of sandy beaches has helped level off holiday development.

‘ This maritime tract is rugged, and difficult to be approached, but has very good harbours, and is inhabited by a people who are not inclined to violence. ’

STRABO
The Geography
(*c*54BC–AD24)

Previous page: *Tourists admire the rock tombs at Kaunos*

Left: *Myra's spectacular rock tombs*

Demre (Kale)

Set on a broad alluvial plain, with hothouses on every available inch of land, this rather scruffy town, officially called Kale, is more commonly known as Demre. The modern town has little to offer, but the ancient sites are fascinating (➤ 32).

South of Demre is the seaside village of Çayağzi, built on the ancient harbour of Andriake. It has a pleasant harbour front, with fish restaurants and a landscaped walkway, a small beach, thriving boatyards, and a massive Roman granary, built by Hadrian between AD119 and 139 and used as a central supply depot for the entire empire. In summer boat trips go from here to Kekova and Simena.

- 28B1
- 46km (29miles) east of Kaş, 27km (17 miles) west of Finike; Andriake 3km (2 miles) south of Demre
- *Dolmuş*
- None
- Finike (➤ 36), Kekova (➤ 38)
- Camel-wrestling contests in Jan/Feb (➤ 116)

What to See in Demre

MYRA ✪✪

Myra was one of the earliest and most important of the cities in the Lycian federation, dating back to the 5th century BC. Its name comes from the myrrh tree, whose gum resin was a valuable trading commodity. The ruins, under the cliff behind Demre, include an imposing free-standing theatre which was converted in the 2nd century AD for gladiatorial combat. Look for the fallen frieze of theatrical masks. Behind the theatre are tiers of magnificent Lycian house tombs whose carved friezes and traces of red, blue and purple paint retain but a shadow of their ancient artistry. The *agora*, probably east of the theatre, is still unexcavated, but there are remains of a 5th-century BC fortress on the acropolis above and a further group of tombs to the northeast of the main site, including the so-called 'Painted Tomb'. The paint has faded, but the relief carvings of a family feast are still remarkable.

- 28B1
- 1km (half a mile) north of Demre
- May–end Sep daily 7.30–7; Oct–end Apr daily 8–5.30
- *Dolmuş* to central Demre
- None
- Inexpensive
- Finike (➤ 36), Kekova (➤ 38)

Right: *Remote Arykanda has one of the finest settings of any city*
Below: *Tombs record the lives of their inhabitants*

28B1
Demre centre: clearly signed
Daily 8.30–4.30
Dolmuş
None
Moderate
Finike (➤ 36), Kekova (➤ 38)
Feast of St. Nicholas, 6 December

NOEL BABA KİLESİ 

St. Nicholas (➤ 14) was bishop of Myra in the late 4th and early 5th centuries AD, and the church's roots date from this time. The church was enlarged by Emperor Justinian in the 6th century, before being destroyed by Arab raiders in 1034. It was again restored in 1043, by Constantine IX, and by the Russians in the 1862. In 1087, Nicholas' body was stolen by Italian traders and taken to the 11th-century basilica of San Nicola in Bari, Italy.

In the last decade, flood damage has necessitated major repairs, particularly to its Byzantine frescoes now undergoing restoration, supported by global sponsors. In 2002, the Russian Orthodox Church erected a revolving statue of St. Nicholas here. A service is held here every December as part of the celebrations of St. Nicholas Festival.

What to See in Lycia

ANDRİAKE (DEMRE, ➤ 31–2)

28B2
30km (19 miles) north of Finike, off the Elmalı road (➤ 40–41 for access)

ARYKANDA (ARİF) 

This is one of the most isolated, complete and spectacularly beautiful ancient cities in Lycia. Built vertically at the end of a deep valley, it remains a cool, green haven all year round, but in spring it is particularly decorative, with carpets of flowers, snow-capped mountain peaks and several small waterfalls.

Arykanda was probably founded in the 2nd millennium BC, but the first historic evidence dates to the 5th century BC. As with other Lycian cities, it was ruled successively by the Persians, Alexander, the Seleucids and the Ptolemies, joined the Lycian federation and became Roman in AD43. After earthquakes in the 2nd, 3rd and 5th centuries AD, and Arab invasions in the 7th–8th centuries, the locals finally gave up and moved down the valley.

From the car park, the lower acropolis (to the right) includes the ruins of shops and a small 4th-century AD bath house. The tin-roofed sheds to the left protect the mosaic floors of a large Byzantine basilica. Further up the hill is the entertainment district, with an odeon (for musical performances), theatre, stadium, and the *agora*. The main path leads round to a bath complex, whose 10m- (33-ft) high arched ceilings, picture windows and mosaic floors are nearly intact. Near the cliff face are an arcaded market, a gymnasium, various paved streets and a Roman temple, later adapted for Christian worship. The necropolis is at the far eastern end of the site.

Did you know ?

In 1838–9, a British archaeologist, Sir Charles Fellows, led an expedition to Lycia. He rediscovered the remains of 13 ancient cities, including Tlos and Xanthos (▶ 49). He then stripped them of their finest friezes, sculptures and mosaics, shipping them all back to London. Most of his finds are on display in the British Museum.

- 28A2
- 97km (60 miles) west of Fethiye, 25km (16 miles) off the N-400 at Ortaca
- All sights open access
- *Dolmuş*; access to Kaunos by boat or foot only
- None
- All sights inexpensive

Above: *history the easy way—tourist boats cruise past the Dalyan tombs*

DALYAN AND KAUNOS

The busy little tourist resort of Dalyan is inland, on the east bank of the broad Dalyan Çayı. There are no sights in the town itself, but it is quiet and charming, with several good seafood restaurants along the river. Boat trips provide transport to the local beaches, the nearby mud baths and upriver to Kaunos, passing rock tombs high on the bank.

To the north, the road winds for 13km (8 miles) along a huge freshwater lake, Köyceğiz Gölü. The surrounding swampy reed-beds are alive with birds, dragonflies, butterflies and other wildlife, while weirs (*dalyan* means fishing weir) catch grey mullet and sea bass as they return downstream after breeding. Also upstream, İlıca's smelly thermal mud baths are said to increase male potency and cure gynaecological problems and rheumatism—and they're fun, if not altogether hygienic.

On the coast, İstuzu Beach is a spectacular, 5km (3 mile) stretch of sand with a healthy breeding colony of loggerhead turtles. From April to October (the breeding season) bathers must leave the beach before nightfall. Beach umbrellas are discouraged in case they damage the eggs.

Kaunos, 10km (6 miles) west, is a Hellenistic city, famous for exporting salt and slaves, with 4th-century BC walls and a fort, a 2nd-century BC theatre, a huge Roman bath (in restoration), a Byzantine basilica and several tombs built by the local Carian people in the Lycian style.

The ruins are now 5km (3 miles) inland, the harbour having silted up over the centuries, leaving beautiful reed-beds swarming with terrapins, frogs and flamingoes. Boats dock 10 minutes' walk from the site.

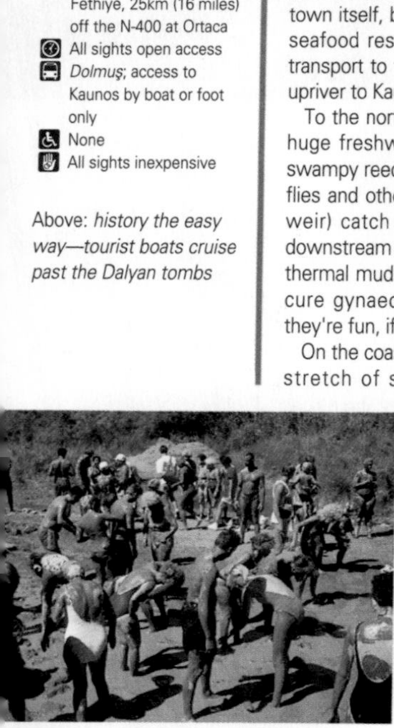

Happy tourists wallowing in Dalyan mud baths

Turkish Delight comes in many flavours

FETHİYE ✪✪

This busy port and market town, tucked into a broad bay at the foot of Mount Crasus, marks both the western border of Lycia and the western end of the Taurus Mountains. It's been here for at least 3,000 years, but has suffered periodic identity crises. Known to the Lycians as Telmessos and to the Byzantines as Anastasiopolis, it became Makri in 1424 under the Ottomans, finally changing its name again in 1923 in memory of a local pilot, Fethi Bey, who died during the War of Independence. It suffered earthquake damage in 1856 and 1957, leaving only a few fragmentary historical remains in a largely modern town.

Although its offshoot beach resorts of Çalış (4km/2 miles west of town) and Ölüdeniz are busy throughout the season, Fethiye still remains, at least in part, a working Turkish town, although the growing foreign population are trying hard to ensure their presence doesn't crowd out the local way of life. Next to the yachts and tourist *gülets* in the marina are small, brightly painted fishing boats and giant freighters, loading chrome and vegetables from the docks where Lycians once loaded frankincense and myrrh.

There are several particularly grand Lycian tombs—in front of the Town Hall near the modern harbour, in the old town and, most magnificent of all, the 4th-century BC **Tomb of Amyntas**, carved into the sheer cliff behind the town. Just behind the tourist office, the amphitheatre is undergoing restoration. On top of the mountain is a ruined fort, thought to have been built in the 14th century by the Crusader Knights of St. John, who were based on nearby Rhodes. Fragmentary Lycian, Greek and Byzantine remains are also visible. The town's small **museum** has archaeological remains from the region. Parks and open-air cafés line the seafront and there are bars and restaurants.

28A2
50km (31 miles) east of Dalaman airport; 225km (140 miles) west of Antalya
İskele Karşasi 1, opposite the main harbour
0252 614 1527
Dolmuş
Boat trips to various local islands; ferries to Rhodes (Greece)
None; access to harbour area
Ölüdeniz (➤ 43), Pınara (➤ 46), Saklıkent (➤ 47), Tlos (➤ 49)
Tueday Farmers' Market is vey popular

Tomb of Amyntas
Up the steps from Kaya Caddesi, behind the bus station
Daily 8.30–sunset
Inexpensive

Museum
Off Atatürk Caddesi
Tue–Sun 8.30–12, 1–5.30
Moderate

28B1
140km (87 miles) southwest of Antalya; 60km (37 miles) southwest of Kemer; 77km (48 miles) east of Kaş (➤ 40–1 for details of directions to Limyra)
Open access
Some restaurants (£–££)
Dolmuş to Finike and Turunçova (3km/2 miles from Limyra)
None
Free

Above: *Every available inch of land is crowded with orchards and greenhouses*

Opposite: *Kalkan's pretty harbour*

FİNİKE AND LİMYRA

Finike, known to the ancients as Phoenicus, was an important port for the export of timber. Isolated during Ottoman times, it was a fishing and agricultural village. Today, its fortunes are based on fruit, with luscious honeydew melons in summer, sweet winter oranges, and huge, tasty tomatoes all year round. There are several fine old Ottoman buildings and a well-equipped marina, overlooked by several restaurants. Careful planning has kept tourism development relatively low key, making it an ideal place for an inexpensive, quiet holiday immersed in Turkish culture.

Ruined Limyra, 8km (5 miles) north, was the capital of King Pericles (founder of the Lycian federation) in the 4th century BC. It later became a Byzantine bishopric, but was abandoned after heavy damage during 7th- to 9th-century Arab raids. Many of the buildings are scattered through the modern village, often doubling as garden walls. The almost square buildings near the river were part of a Byzantine convent; to the left is an imposing 2nd-century AD theatre. Above all, this is the site of the largest necropolis in Lycia: the stony hillside is peppered with tombs, from the simple to the grandiose. One of the most elaborate is the free-standing 4th-century BC tomb of Xantabura, just beyond the theatre, its reliefs depicting a funeral banquet and the judgement of the dead. Right at the top, involving a severe 40-minute scramble, is the Heroön, the tomb of Pericles himself, its frieze showing scenes from the life of the hero.

KALKAN ✪✪✪

Kalkan has long been considered the quiet little sister to Kaş, and the prettiest of the small coastal resorts. Until 1923 it was a Greek village that made a poor living from fishing, charcoal-burning and olives. Today, its simple cottages have been beautifully restored and redeveloped as delightful shops, restaurants and *pansiyons*. Built down the side of a deep valley, its narrow, bougainvillea-draped streets tumbling into a tiny harbour (now a smart marina), it's a very upmarket place with excellent food and shopping and easy access to numerous historic sights. Building now extends to all the surrounding hills and hinterland. The local beaches are man made; the nearest natural sand beaches are tiny Kaputaş (6km/4 miles east), shared with Kaş, and vast Patara (19km/11 miles west).

- 28A1
- 26km (22 miles) west of Kaş, on the N-400
- Wide choice (£–££)
- *Dolmuş*
- None
- Kaş (➤ 21), Patara (➤ 23), Kekova (➤ 38), Demre (➤ 31), Letoön (➤ 42), Phellos (➤ 45), Pınara (➤ 46), Saklıkent and Sidyma (➤ 47), Tlos and Xanthos (➤ 49)

KARAİN MAĞARASI (KARAIN CAVE) ✪✪

Rediscovered by Guiseppe Moretti (➤ 64) in 1919, Karain was an ideal home: a healthy, south-facing cave 370m (1,214ft) above sea level and a safe 80m (262ft) above the plain, with a good water supply and a rich local food supply. The first humans moved in about 30,000 years ago, and it remained inhabited for 20,000 years. The cave has proved to be the single most important prehistoric site in Turkey, producing fascinating finds, from hippopotamus bones to arrowheads and the skull of a Neanderthal child. There are three large caverns: the first two were used for living, the third as a place of refuge, a cemetery and, during the classical period, as a temple. All three have stalactites and stalagmites. There are stairs, proper lighting and a small but detailed site museum.

- 28B2
- 27km (23 miles) northwest of Antalya, off the N-650 to Burdur; the cave is about 6km (4 miles) from the main road
- Daily 8.30–5
- None
- Inexpensive
- Termessos (➤ 48)
- Many finds are in the Museum of Anatolian Civilizations in Ankara and the Antalya Archaeological Museum (➤ 17)

KAŞ (➤ 21, TOP TEN)

28A2
7km (4 miles) south of Fethiye
Open access
None
Free
Ölüdeniz (➤ 43)

Above: *Boatman amongst the submerged Lycian tombs of ancient Simena*

KAYAKÖY

Kaya (which means 'rocky village') is an eery complete ghost village on the site of ancient Karmylassos. Until 1923, it was a thriving village of around 3,500 people, most of them Greek Orthodox, who had settled here from the Dodecanese. In 1923 they were deported, along with nearly a million others. The Macedonian Muslims who were shipped into Turkey in the massive exchange of population believed Kaya to be cursed, and it was abandoned. Around 400 houses still cling, roofless, to the hillside. In 2002, it became a UNESCO World Heritage Site and will be restored as an historic settlement. There are a few *pansiyons*, a wine house and the beginnings of prosperity.

28B1
30km (19 miles) east of Kaş by road; turn off the N-400 and follow signs for 19km (12 miles) to Üçağız; or there's a direct 25km (16 miles) road from Demre to Üçağız
In season, there are regular full-day *gület* trips to Kekova from Kaş, Kalkan and Andriake (Demre)
Good fish restaurants in Üçağız and Simena (£–££)
Simena castle inexpensive; boat trip expensive
Kaş (➤ 21)

KEKOVA ADASI (ISLAND)

A boat trip to the long, skinny island of Kekova is one of the most popular excursions on the Lycian coast. Tours start in Kaş or Demre, or drive to the tiny harbour in Üçağız, a pretty little village with a few shops, restaurants and simple *pansiyons*, and negotiate with a local fisherman. On the rocks to the east, all that remains of the ancient city of Teimiussa is a Lycian necropolis, with some partly submerged tombs.

Around the headland, Kale (ancient Simena) is accessible only by water. The harbour is like a postcard, with several waterfront restaurants and women selling crafts. To reach the castle at the top is a steep climb, but worth it for the view, which is magical. Within the crenellated walls is the smallest theatre in Lycia, with just 300 seats.

The Byzantine Batık Şehir (Sunken City), drowned after a massive earthquake. The remains of the harbour foundations, walls and ruined sarcophagi are visible both above and below the water line. Swimming and diving

are allowed and there are also other excellent swimming and snorkelling stops, such as Tersane, a small bay with a pebble beach, ruined Byzantine chapel and monastery. Beware of sea urchins, it is best to wear shoes. Some of the smaller boats may also sail right inside to see a local sea cave.

KEMER

As proud owner of one of the first stretches of really good beach west of Antalya, Kemer is the hub of one of the most intensively developed stretches of the Turkish Riviera. The town itself is pleasantly small with enough Turkish people, supermarkets and orange groves to remind one of the real world. On the seafront, a host of luxury hotels and restaurants and an aquapark line the little beach and the smartly restored marina that is the focus of local life. There are also strips of giant hotels at nearby Göynük, Beldibi, Çamyuva and Tekirova. There are, however, surprisingly few entertainment facilities on offer locally; everything is provided by the all-inclusive resorts and many guests never leave their hotel grounds.

Below: *Kemer's marina is as crowded as its beaches with glamorous yachts from all around Europe*

- 28B2
- 45km (28 miles) south-west of Antalya on the N-400
- Belediye ve Turizm Binası (under the Town Hall) 0242 814 1537
- Choice of restaurants (£)
- *Dolmuş* from Antalya, outside the Sheraton, Falez and Octogon hotels
- None
- Phaselis (➤ 26), Olympos (➤ 44), Antalya (➤ 53)

The Apple Blossom Tour

Distance
360km (223 miles)

Time
1 very full day; preferably 2 days. Go in Mar/Apr for blossoms. It is possible to stay overnight in Finike, but this is the last suitable point until you reach Antalya

Start/end point
Kemer
28B2

Lunch
At one of several small roadside restaurants near Arykanda, or at a café in Elmalı (£)

This magnificent circular drive encompasses all that is finest about Lycia. The first section, to Finike, follows the coast road; the next, as far as Elmalı, crosses the wild passes of the Taurus Mountains. The section from Elmalı to Korkuteli offers a rare glimpse of the high plains of inland Anatolia, and the last stretch to Antalya again meanders through forested mountains. There are numerous sights along the way, but the scenery is the real star. The drive is feasible in one day only if the more accessible sights are left for another occasion.

Leave Kemer on the N-400 heading south, past the turnings for Phaselis (➤ 26), Olympos and the Chimaera (➤ 44). At Finike (➤ 36), 71km (44 miles) from Kemer, turn on to the N-635 to Elmalı and Korkuteli.

The 15th-century Ömerpaşa Camii in Elmalı has a finely tiled porch

Almost immediately, the coastal development gives way to peasant farms, with ramshackle old houses amongst the apple orchards and lemon groves, shaggy goats and chickens scratching in the verges, women in baggy trousers and cardigans working in the fields.

After 7km (4 miles), in Turunçova, turn right to Limyra (➤ 36), 3km (2 miles) off the main road. The signs peter out, but keep going as straight as possible. Just after you think you have taken a wrong turning, you see the first of the ruins. Return to the main road.

The main road continues north, past another group of rock tombs, winding along the milky turquoise Akçay River valley through spectacular pine-clad mountains. There are plenty of viewing points, but concentration is required, as brightly decorated fruit lorries tend to hurl themselves round the bends in a suicidal fashion.

After 21km (13 miles), just beyond the pass, is the tiny mountain village of Arif. Look for a yellow sign to Arykanda (➤ 32), hidden round a blind

corner. The site is 1km (half a mile) off the main road along a rough track, just passable by car, with limited parking. To turn safely, go to the restaurant, turn round, then take the track on the left. If possible, leave your car at the restaurant and walk.

Back on the main road, keep going north through Göltana (a huge, shallow lake surrounded by snow-capped peaks in winter, and a broad, dry pan in summer), for 38km (24 miles) to Elmalı.

This busy market town on the slopes of 2,296m (7,530ft) Elmalı Dağ (Apple Mountain) has a beautiful 15th-century mosque, the Ömerpaşa Camii, together with a number of fine, timber-framed Ottoman mansions. This is a crucially important area for Anatolian prehistory, with major Bronze Age settlements at nearby Karataş-Semayük and painted chamber tombs at Kızılbel and Karaburun, all within a 10km (6 miles) radius of the town. None are open to the public; some of the finds, including exquisite gold, silver and bronze jewellery and ivory figurines, are in the Antalya Archaeological Museum (Antalya Müzesi, ➤ 17).

From Elmalı, head north to Korkuteli (52km/32 miles), then turn right on to the N-350 past the Karain Cave (➤ 37) and Termessos (➤ 48) to Antalya (➤ 53–56), where you turn south, back on to the N-400 back to Kemer (45km/28 miles).

Bees feast on the spring flowers to produce fine honey with rich overtones of Mediterranean herbs

28A1
26km (16 miles) west of Kalkan, off the N-400. The turn-off is 1.5km (1 mile) west of Kınık; the site is about 4km (2.5miles) from the main road
May–end Sep daily 7.30–7; Oct–end Apr daily 8.30–5
Dolmuş to main road turn-off
None, reasonable access
Inexpensive
Kaş (➤ 21), Patara (➤ 23), Kalkan (➤ 37), Pınara (➤ 46), Saklıkent and Sidyma (➤ 47) Tlos and Xanthos (➤ 49)

LETOÖN

According to legend, the goddess Leto fled here from Mount Olympos to protect her twin babies, Apollo and Artemis, from Zeus's jealous wife, Hera. Local shepherds tried to drive her away, but she was aided by friendly wolves, in whose honour she changed the name of the area to Lycia (after *lykos*, Greek for wolf). She then turned the shepherds into frogs. Leto, Apollo and Artemis became the ruling deities of Lycia.

This charming little temple complex probably began as a site sacred to the Mother Goddess before the 7th century BC. It later became the place of assembly (parliament) of the Lycian federation. Today, there are three temples dedicated to Leto (2nd century BC, to the right), Artemis (4th or 5th century BC, in the centre) and Apollo (1st century BC, to the left), with a fine mosaic floor. Behind are a nymphaeum (fountain) and Byzantine basilica, in front various Roman buildings, including a small Hellenistic theatre. Many remain flooded for much of the year and are more like an aquarium than a Roman ruin, with huge numbers of frogs (shepherds?), terrapins, ducks and other waterbirds.

LİMYRA (FINİKE, ➤ 36)

28A2
146km (91 miles) west of Fethiye
İskele Meydanı 2
0252 313 0722
Dolmuş or coach
None
All sights inexpensive
Tango festival in Sep

MARMARİS

The huge, fjord-like bay at Marmaris, backed by steep, pine-clad mountains, once housed the ancient Dorian port of Physus. Little remains of this, but the natural deep-water harbour has attracted many notable sailors, including Süleyman the Magnificent who, in 1522, built a formidable, squat fortress (now an ethnographic museum) while preparing his successful attack on Rhodes. In 1798, Lord Nelson sheltered the British fleet here before defeating Napoleon in the Battle of the Nile. Marmaris is now a popular yachting centre, with a world-class marina attracting a fabulous array of gin palaces alongside the local *gülets*. The attractive town also has a pleasant seafront promenade, excellent restaurants, various international yachting events and a great bazaar. The larger tourist hotels are strung out along the beach at İçmeler (west) and Turunç (south).

Lying on the scenic peninsula west of Marmaris are the popular little resort of Datça (76km/47 miles) and the vast, largely unexcavated ruins of ancient Knidos (100km/62 miles). Best to visit by boat.

Outdoor dining—on the Marmaris waterfront—a great treat

MYRA (DEMRE, ➤ 31)

➤ 31

ÖLÜDENİZ ✪✪✪

Freely acknowledged to be one of the most beautiful lagoons in the Mediterranean, Ölüdeniz (Dead Sea) was formed by a long spit of sand almost blocking off a circular bay. Steep, heavily forested mountains sweep down to the deep, blue water, while the sand spit provides acres of sunbathing. Keep a close eye on children, as the sand at Belcekız Beach drops rapidly away from the shore. A small area immediately around the lagoon has been designated a national park, but unfortunately most of the sand spit is a car park, and the valley leading down to the sea is wall-to-wall hotels and holiday homes. The beaches are busy and crowded in summer, but there is ample greenery and a congenial atmosphere. If you prefer peace and quiet, stay at one of the many hotels set in forested areas only a few kilometres inland. Ölüdeniz is now an important paragliding centre—watch the tandem teams landing on the soft sand.

- 28A2
- 20km (12 miles) south of Fethiye
- Open access
- Many restaurants and cafés in the village (££)
- *Dolmuş* from Fethiye
- None
- Moderate
- Fethiye (➤ 35), Pınara (➤ 46), Saklıkent (➤ 47), Tlos (➤ 49)

Above: *The magnificent turquoise lagoon at Ölüdeniz is one of the finest sights along a spectacular coast*

Left: *Antique and reproduction Ottoman coffee pots are sold in the Marmaris bazaar*

- 28B1
- 35km (22 miles) south of Kemer; the first turning off the main road leads to the Chimaera, the second to Olympos
- Open access
- Çıralı has many inexpensive *pansiyons* and restaurants; also several near Olympos and nearby Ulupinar (££)
- *Dolmuş* to the Olympos turn-off or Çıralı village; in season, shuttle buses and taxis depart from a café 2km (1 mile) west of the turn off
- From Kemer and Antalya, in season
- None
- Olympos: moderate; Chimaera: free
- Phaselis (➤ 26)

Flames leap from the ground at the extraordinary Chimaera

OLYMPOS AND THE CHİMAERA

Make every effort to reach these fascinating sights. From the main road there are two turnings. The first (northerly) turning, just before the bridge, leads for 9km (6 miles) through the village of Çıralı to the base of the hill, from where it is a 30-minute walk up to the Chimaera. The second (southerly) turning, beside the café just beyond the bridge, is 11km (7 miles) long and leads directly to Olympos. Both routes involve some dirt tracks that may not be passable in winter. It is possible to walk along the pebble beach between Çıralı and Olympos in summer (allow 15 minutes).

By the 2nd century BC, Olympos was one of the more important cities of the Lycian Federation. Conquered by Cilician pirates in the 1st century BC, it was freed by Pompey in 67BC and became part of the Roman Empire in AD43. It was eventually abandoned after the Ottomans took control in the 15th century.

Today, it is a tranquil haven on the river mouth between high cliffs, filled with flowers, birds, frogs and turtles. The partially excavated ruins cover an extraordinary range of history, from Lycian tombs near the harbour, to a Roman theatre and baths, a Byzantine basilica, and 11th- to 12th-century Genoese fortifications. Nearby are the timbered remains of abandoned chromium mines; chrome was used in the tanning of leather hides.

The Chimaera (best seen at dusk) is a natural phenomenon: a series of flames spouting out of the bare hillside, thought to be fed by natural methane gas and named after the mythical monster said to inhabit these hills. According to Homer, she had the head of a lion, the body of a goat and the tail of a serpent, and breathed fire. Bellerophon, on his trusty steed, Pegasus, had to slay her to win the hand of the King of Lycia's daughter. Early Olympians worshipped Hephaestus (Vulcan), the god of fire, whose shrine is nearby. The Cilicians introduced the worship of Mithras, the Zoroastrian god of light, whose ceremonies also involved the flames. The best part of Olympos is its tranquil setting, abundant wildlife and superb beach. The surrounding mountains are part of the Beydağlar Olympos National Park, with good hiking.

PATARA (➤ 23, TOP TEN)

PHASELİS (➤ 26, TOP TEN)

PHELLOS

This virtually unexcavated site or 'stony place' has fine views and the substantial remains of an ancient Lycian settlement. To reach it, take the N-400 towards Antalya, turn left after about 11km (7 miles) at Ağullu to the village of Çukurbağ. Continue up a driveable track for 5km (3 miles) until the road ends at the forest lookout station. It is then a 30-minute walk to the site. Stretches of fortified city wall still stand, along with vast, elaborate house tombs, the remains of a temple and several wells that are still in use. The mountain walk and the accompanying magnificent views are as much of an attraction as the ruins.

28B1
About 20km (12 miles) north of Kaş
Open access
None
Free
Kaş (➤ 21)

After the ruins, head for the beach at Olympos

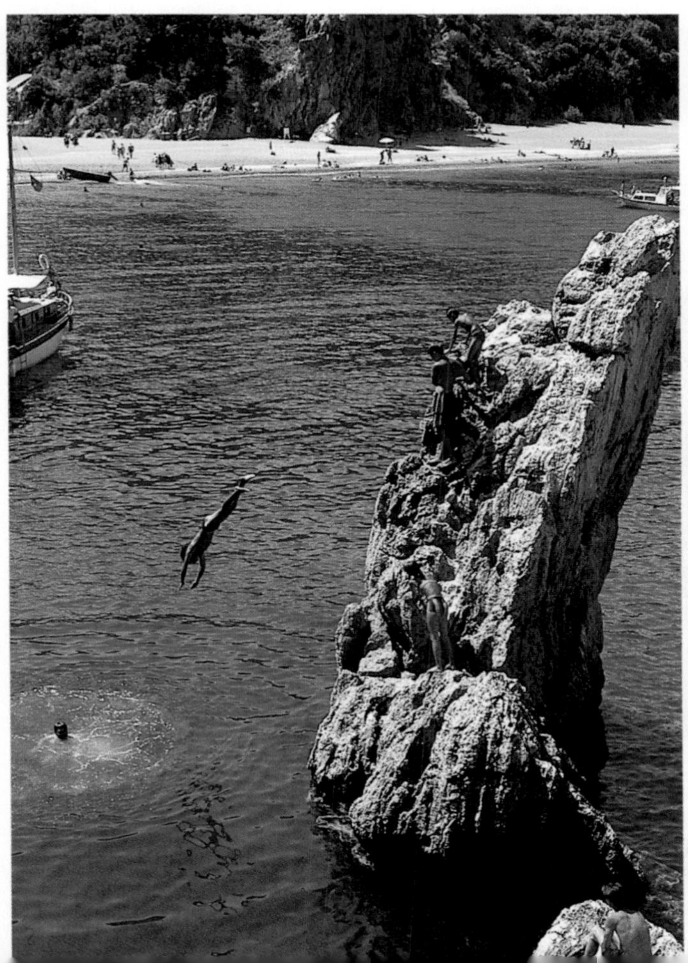

28A2
50km (31 miles) southeast of Fethiye, off the N-400; 3km (2 miles) from turn-off through Minare village, then a 30-minute walk
Open access, officially daily 8.30–6
Dolmuş to turning off main road
None
Inexpensive
Letoön (➤ 42), Saklıkent, Sidyma (➤ 47), Tlos and Xanthos (➤ 49)

PINARA

This is a difficult site to reach, but well worth it. The 4km (2.5 miles) dirt track leading up to it from the village of Minare emphasizes the strategic location of Pinara and the independent spirit of its inhabitants. Another of the great cities of the Lycian Federation, it was probably founded as an offshoot colony of Xanthos (➤ 49). The ruins are unexcavated and overgrown, but the site is dramatic, dominated by a 500m (1640ft) red cliff. A difficult path leads to the top, where there are a few remains of the earliest town. The east face is honeycombed with often highly sophisticated Lycian tombs so inaccessible that their builders had to be lowered on ropes. The smaller hill to the east is the site of the later city. This also has a number of rock tombs, including the elaborate Royal Tomb, with reliefs depicting four walled cities and a festival, plus an *agora*, temple and theatre.

28B1
56km (35 miles) southwest of Kemer, off the N-400; 3km (2 miles) north of Kumluca via Hacıveliler or Seyköy
Open access
Dolmuş to Kumluca
None Free
Phaselis (➤ 26), Limyra (➤ 36), Olympos and the Chimaera (➤ 44)

RHODİAPOLİS

Reaching this remote site involves either an hour's walk through mountain forests, or a four-by-four vehicle; the access track is not suitable for ordinary cars. However, the walk is the biggest treat. Using a local guide is sensible.

Rhodiapolis was a Lycian city. Sadly, its ruins, much damaged by vandals and fortune-hunters, are now scattered across the pine forest. At the centre is a well-preserved theatre; to the south are the ravaged remains of the vast, elaborate Tomb of Opramoas, a 2nd-century AD philanthropist of note, covered in sculpture and inscriptions recording the many honours bestowed on him for his charitable work throughout the Roman Empire.

Lycian rock tombs—this time at Pınara

SAKLIKENT ✪✪

The attraction here is a cool, dark, narrow gorge, about 300m (984ft) high and 18km (11 miles) long, carved out by the icy churning waters of the Eşen River.

Access to the gorge is by a suspended wooden catwalk. To cover the full length of the gorge requires the proper expeditionary equipment, organization and mountaineering skills. If you want a different kind of sport, you'll find that it is also a popular and challenging place for abseiling.

For the less intrepid, restaurants at the base of the gorge are known for their fresh-cooked trout from local hatcheries. In summer the Turks come here escape the gruelling heat and wallow in the cool, green calm.

- 28A1
- 36km (22 miles) east of Fethiye, off the N-350 to Korkuteli; 3km (2 miles) from main road
- Open access
- Several restaurants downstream (£–££)
- None
- Free
- Fethiye (➤ 35), Tlos and Xanthos (➤ 49)

SIDYMA (DODURGA) ✪

Sidyma was a coastal city, dating back to at least the 2nd century BC, whose ruins are scattered among the houses of modern Dodurga and across the surrounding hills. The mosque, built reusing ancient stones, has inscriptions to the pagan gods on the back wall. There is also a necropolis, a badly damaged theatre and a few remains of the *agora* and temple.

- 28A1
- 29km (18 miles) north of Kalkan, about 7km (4 miles) off the N-400 to Fethiye (about 50km/31 miles) from Fethiye), but you can only access Sidyma from Eşen, not from Kalkan
- Open access
- None
- Free
- Patara (➤ 23), Letoön (➤ 42), Pınara (➤ 46), Xanthos (➤ 49)

Did you know ?

The distinctive Lycian tombs (now all empty) were designed as family residences for the afterlife and probably closely mirrored domestic architecture of the period. Bodies were buried with a full range of possessions. In some cases, inscriptions give details of the inhabitants' lives, while the most important had relief carvings outside and frescoes inside.

Above: *The setting of Pınara theatre has as much drama as any performance on its stage*

Above: *Magnificent views at Termessos*

SİMENA (KEKOVA, ➤ 38)

TERMESSOS

28B2

37km (23 miles) northwest of Antalya, off the N-350 to Korkuteli. Turn after 30km (19 miles); the car park is about 9km (6 miles) from the main road up a forest track. Exploration involves a further, steep, 2km (1 mile) walk. Stout shoes and lots of water

Daily 8–7

Dolmuş to the turning off the main road

None Inexpensive

Antalya (➤ 53), Karain Mağarası (➤ 37), Apple Blossom Tour (➤ 40)

Termessos, or 'Eagle's Nest', lies in a magnificent position high in the mountains (1,650m/5,412ft), just within ancient Pisidia, guarding its borders with Lycia and Pamphylia.

The people of the city, fiercely warlike indigenous Anatolians, lived on the olive harvest and what they could take off others, both by demanding heavy tolls from passing travellers and a sideline in banditry. In 334BC, they distinguished themselves by beating off Alexander, who was forced to move on after burning their olive groves. The city prospered during the Hellenistic years and from 70BC to the 3rd century AD, retaining independence under Roman patronage. It was abandoned after a massive earthquake in AD527. The overgrown, unexcavated ruins include a 4,200-seat theatre with a fabulous setting, the *agora*, a colonnaded street, an odeon, four temples, one dedicated to Zeus Solymeus, and a necropolis with nearly 1,000 tombs.

The surrounding area, including the dramatic Göksu Kanyon, is now protected from development as the Güllükdağı Termessos Milli Parkı (national park), which has dense forests, butterflies and wild plants and is one of the last refuges for the Anatolian lynx.

Nearby Döşmealtı village has a high reputation as a weaving centre, producing magnificent carpets in strong, earthy colours and geometric designs.

TLOS

This is one of Lycia's longest inhabited cities, mentioned in 14th-century BC Hittite documents, whose Ottoman castle (built over the Lycian fortress) was still inhabited in the 19th centuryby the vicious pirate Kanlı Ali Ağa (Bloody Ali). The rock outcrop below the castle has numerous Lycian house tombs, including the elaborate Tomb of Bellerophon, slayer of the Chimaera (➤ 44), depicting the hero riding winged Pegasus. The local royal family claimed descent. The flatter land leading down to the Eşen River was the site of a prosperous Roman city, whose remains include the *agora*, market hall, stadium, baths, a theatre, and sections of the city wall. In Byzantine times, Tlos was a bishopric and a small church remains from this era.

28A2
36km (22 miles) east of Fethiye; turn off the N-350 to Korkuteli after 22km (14 miles) and follow signs to Yakaköy
Open access
None
Inexpensive
Kalkan (➤ 37), Kaş (➤ 21), Patara (➤ 23), Letoön (➤ 42), Pınara (➤ 46), Saklıkent and Sidyma (➤ 47), Xanthos (➤ 49)

Left: *Only a few miles from the coast, traditional lifestyles continue*

Bottom left: *The wonderful theatre at Termessos is part of the landscape*

UÇAĞIZ (KEKOVA, ➤ 38)

XANTHOS

Xanthos was the capital and single most important city in the Lycian Federation. Its people had such overwhelming pride that twice they totally destroyed the city rather than submit to a conqueror. In 545BC, when besieged by the Persian general, Harpagos, the warriors slaughtered their families and slaves, then torched the city before the final battle. In 42BC, when Roman Brutus arrived to collect funds for his war with Octavian and Mark Anthony, they did the same thing. Only about 150 survived as captives. The following year, Mark Anthony helped them rebuild their city, which prospered as capital of Roman Lycia.

The imposing ruins combine Lycian, Persian and Greek styles. Start partway up the hill with the 1st-century AD Arch of Vespasian, a Hellenistic gateway and the Nereid monument (about AD4), now denuded of its decorative friezes. On the main outcrop stands a Roman theatre and *agora* and several pillar tombs (found only at Xanthos), including a Lycian tomb perched on a column, the 7.6m (25ft), 5th-century BC Harpy Tomb, with replica reliefs, and the Inscribed Pillar, recounting the life of a 5th-century BC prince, Kerei. On the acropolis are the remains of the earliest city (8th century BC), and a Byzantine monastery. The missing artwork was all removed by Sir Charles Fellows in 1838 and is now in the British Museum.

28A1
26km northwest of Kalkan. The turn-off is in the centre of Kınık townor signposted a few kilometres west off the main road to Fethiye
Open access; officially May–end Oct daily 8–7; Nov–end Apr daily 8–7,30
Café in the car park
Dolmuş to Kınık
None
Inexpensive
Kalkan (➤ 37), Kaş (➤ 21), Patara (➤ 23), Letoön (➤ 42), Pınara (➤ 46), Saklıkent and Sidyma (➤ 47), Tlos (➤ 49)

Food & Drink

Coffee
Coffee was introduced to the Turkish court in 1555 by two Syrian traders. By the late 17th century, the Sultan had his own coffee-maker, with 40 assistants, and the women in the harem were given intensive training in its preparation. It is an important element of hospitality: one local proverb says that 'a cup of coffee commits one to 40 years of friendship'. After finishing and draining your cup, it is said you can read your fortune in the coffee grounds.

Above: *Turkish pastries are sticky, calorific and utterly delicious*

Below: *Turkish Delight, one of Turkey's most famous exports*

With the growing popularity of the healthy Mediterranean diet, the basics of Turkish cuisine are surprisingly familiar to many visitors.

A typical meal begins with a choice of *meze* (small starters), including yoghurt with garlic and (maybe) coriander; *houmous* (a dip made from sesame oil and chickpeas); various aubergine and spinach dishes, *dolma* (vine leaves stuffed with rice, pinenuts, currants and herbs), and shepherd's salad, a sharply refreshing blend of tomato and cucumber, onion and green pepper, with a simple dressing of lemon, coriander and Turkey's excellent olive oil.

Main Courses

Fundamental to the diet is the kebab, which comes in many guises: the *şişkebabı* (shish kebab), cubed lamb or chicken grilled on a skewer over charcoal with pepper, onion and tomato; the *döner kebab*, with a huge joint or layered slab slowly spit-roasted and thinly sliced as required; the *köfte kebab*, flattened meatballs grilled on a skewer and served with a hot tomato sauce, and local specialities such as the *adaner kebab*—a long skewer wrapped in hot, spicy minced lamb or beef.

Alternative main courses include simply grilled meat or fish and a variety of stews, most containing some of the key local ingredients of lamb, chicken, tomato, onion, peppers, aubergines, beans and chickpeas. *Pilav* (rice) is usually served with meat dishes

In the east, the bread is usually *pide*, a pitta-style flat bread, sometimes served topped with vegetables or minced lamb as a type of pizza (*lahmacun*). Another popular and delicious snack is *börek*, layers of thin pastry stuffed with minced lamb, cheese, spinach or other vegetables.

Desserts

Desserts are rare: the meal ends with fruit or simply with tea or coffee. Cakes, pastries and confectionery abound, but are sold separately in pastry shops (*pastahanes*). Many are variations on the well-known *baklava*, flaky pastry filled with crushed nuts (pistachio, walnut or almond) and drenched in honey or syrup. There are also milky puddings (*muhallabi*) such as *sutlaç* (rice pudding with cinnamon and rosewater) and *keşkül* (a paste of milk, almonds and pistachio, topped with coconut). In Antakya the speciality is *künefe*, a syrupy cheesecake (a cross between Welsh rarebit and *crême brûlée*). The most famous confectionery is, of course, dusted Turkish Delight (*lokum*), which comes flavoured with pistachio, lemon or rosewater.

Drinks

Alcohol is surprisingly free-flowing for a Muslim society, even away from the tourist areas. The local lager, Efes Pilsen, has become a successful export item; there is a dark ale version of it too. 'Troy' is another very passable local brew. The spirit of choice, *rakı*, is an aniseed drink similar to *ouzo* or Pernod. There are some reasonable Turkish wines: most grapes are grown on the Aegean coast or in central Anatolia. The more well-known labels include Yakut, Villa Doluca, Sevilen and Dikmen. Beware the steep prices.

Non-alcoholic options include fresh fruit juices and *ayran*, a thin, slightly salty, yoghurt drink which is both refreshing and an excellent antidote to hot chilli. Tea (*çay*) or strong Turkish coffee (*kahve*) are served black, strong and very sweet, in tiny glasses, as are various herbal or aromatic teas such as apple tea (*elma çay*).

Top: *Heaps of olives, feta cheese and tiny glasses of tea—key ingredients of Turkish cuisine*

Above: *Sun-ripened peaches, fresh from the tree*

Pamphylia

It is hard to imagine, but in 500BC Pamphylia, ruled from Side, was less significant than neighbouring Lycia and Cilicia, although by the 2nd century BC, Side had become a haven for pirates who made a handsome living from slave trading. Its wealth grew further when the Romans poured money into the architectural infrastructure of Perge and Aspendos. Today, its coffers are filled by large expanses of beach-lined coastal plain, ideal for large-scale tourist development, with giant resort hotels creeping together to form unbroken lines many kilometres long and the few spaces between filled with holiday homes.

Near Pamphylia's western border, Antalya, southern Turkey's tourist capital, is fringed by the 12-km (7-mile) hotel strip of Lara. At its eastern edge stand Alanya and the parade of giant resorts at İncekum. Between them are the three great ancient settlements of Perge, Aspendos and Side. The coastal scenery is duller than Lycia's, but there are long, golden beaches and inland are the mountainous delights of the Köprülü Kanyon.

'This country... is one of the finest regions of the world.'

IBN BATTUTA, Arab traveller
(1325–54)

Antalya

Ever since Antalya was built, travellers such as the 14th-century Arab explorer, Ibn Battuta, the 19th-century British sea captain, Sir Francis Beaufort, and 1950s explorer, Freya Stark, have praised its outstanding beauty.

Antalya harbour, once the pride of the Ottomans, is now a tourist jewel of the Turkish Riviera

Antalya was founded in 158BC by King Attalus II of Pergamon. It became Roman, bequeathed to the empire by Attalus III in 133BC, then came under Byzantine control, and was used as a staging post by the Crusaders until it was eventually conquered by the Seljuks in 1206. In the 1390s, the Ottomans took control and it remained their property until 1918, when it was given to Italy in the post-war carve-up of the empire. Only four years later, Atatürk threw out all foreigners, but the Italians had already imbued their quarter with an elegance and dedication to the good life. Today, Antalya has a population of nearly two million. It's a busy port, with an international airport, and has become a dynamic tourist resort. Its setting is magnificent, tucked into a bowl surrounded by the snow-capped peaks of the Taurus Mountains and fronted by a long, curving bay and deep turquoise sea. The old city centre is atmosphereic, although only a fraction of the charming old *konaks* (mansion houses) have been restored.

The main beach, Konyaaltı Plajı, along the western edge of town, has a a smart boardwalk, with walkways, bicycle paths, cafés and playground facilities. Outside Antalya, the most popular beaches are Büyük Çaltıcak and Küçük Çaltıcak, to the west.

What to See in Antalya

ANTALYA MÜZESİ (➤ 17, TOP TEN)

KALEİÇİ ✪✪✪

28B2
Near the Clock Tower
☎ 0242 241 1747
Open access
Choice of cafés, bars and restaurants (£–£££)
Dolmuş, taxi; tramway from museum to Dedeman Hotel
None; streets steep
Free

In 1671 Turkish traveller, Evliya Çelebi described the city of Antalya as being totally surrounded by a wall 4,400m (14,432ft) long, with 80 towers and four gates. Inside it was divided into four quarters, accessed by a further 22 gates, each containing 1,000 houses. One quarter was for the Greeks, one for the Jewish, one for the Muslims, and one for the king, his court and the Mamelukes (ruling class).

In the early 1980s, the old walled town of Kaleiçi (meaning citadel) was spectacularly redeveloped. The main docks had long since moved to Setur, 10km (6 miles) west, and the harbour was converted to a glitzy marina, its quay lined with restaurants. At the far western end is a small, modern amphitheatre, used for live performances in summer. Above it, the old town is a steep rabbit warren of narrow streets and Ottoman mansions (konaks). Some have been converted into carpet shops, restaurants and pansiyons, or restored as private dwellings; many remain much as their previous owners left them. The best way to explore is on foot. Start at the top and work down to the harbour, where there are plenty of cafés, and taxis to take the faint-hearted back up the hill.

Heavily fortified walls protect Antalya's old harbour, now a marina for pleasure boats and yachts

About halfway down on the right is the Yivli Minare (Fluted Minaret, ➤ 56). A little further down, on the left, you will find the Karatay Medrese (religious school), with a beautifully carved triumphal entrance, built in 1250 by a Seljuk vizier.

At the eastern end of the quay, a quick but brutal flight of stairs climbs the cliff, from where a path leads to the mysterious Hıdırlık Kulesi, a 13.45m (44ft) round tower on a square base at the harbour entrance. Built in the 2nd century AD, it has been variously described as a lighthouse, a fort and also a tomb.

Behind this, Hesapçi Sok heads straight into the old residential area, a maze of tiny streets and alleys overhung by rickety wooden-frame houses. A few blocks up on the right is a minaret, all that now remains of the Kesik Minare Camii (Mosque of the Truncated Minaret), destroyed by fire in 1851. It stands on the site formerly occupied by a Roman temple.

A couple of blocks further, on the right, is the Suna-İnan Kiraç (➤ 56). Hadrian's Gate, in Atatürk Caddesi, is a stately marble triple arch, built to welcome Emperor Hadrian in AD130; it marks the eastern edge of Kaleiçi.

Restored Ottoman houses in Kaleiçi, with formidable walls surrounding courtyard gardens

There are excellent views of the old town's painted roofs and the sparkling harbour below from Kalekapısı Square, site of the Clock Tower. This was built in 1244 as part of the main city fortifications, and is now one of Antalya's best-known landmarks. It's an excellent aid to navigation, standing right in the heart of the city at the entrance to the old town. Beside it, to the left, is the 18th-century Tekeli Mehmet Paşa Camii (mosque). To the right, on Cumhuriyet Square, is the magnificent Atatürk Monument. Every town in Turkey has a compulsory statue dedicated to the great leader: Antalya has two and this is one of Turkey's finest.

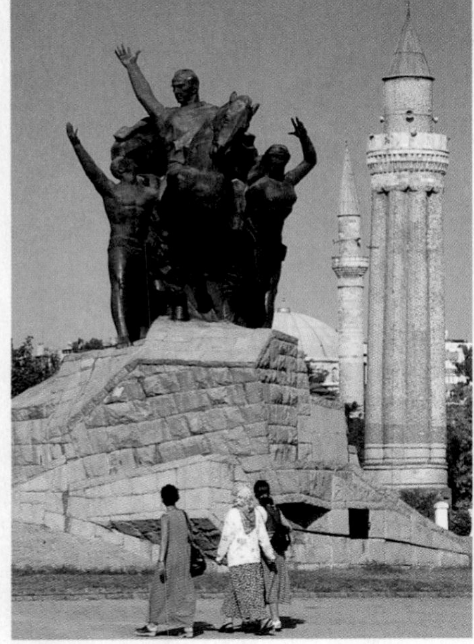

Old and new symbols of a city: Antalya's memorial to Atatürk in front of the Yivli Minare

MINICITY ANTALYA (➤ 110) ✪

SUNA-İNAN KİRAÇ (RESEARCH INSTITUTE) ✪✪

Two beautiful buildings, a two-storey Ottoman mansion and the Greek church of Agios Georgios (St. George), behind it, have been impeccably restored and opened as a specialist research institute for the study of the archaeology, history, ethnography and culture of Mediterranean civilizations. There is also exhibition space for items from the Kiraç's extensive collection, regular changing exhibitions and a lovely garden. Well worth a visit.

- 28B2
- Barbaros Mah, Kocatepe Sok 25, Kaleiçi
- 0242 243 4274
- Thu–Tue 9–6
- Café in the museum, many restaurants and cafés nearby (£–£££)
- None Moderate

YİVLİ MİNARE (FLUTED MINARET) ✪✪

Seljuk Sultan Alâeddin Keykubad I (1219–38) was the single greatest builder along the Mediterranean coast, responsible for many fine buildings, including the Alanya Citadel (➤ 16), Alarahan caravansarai (➤ 61) and this beautiful mosque (built in 1230), which has become the symbol of Antalya. The 38-m (125-ft) high brick minaret, with eight fluted sections on a stone base, was decorated with turquoise and dark blue tiles. It stands in the grounds of a mosque built in 1373 by Mehmet Bey. Beside it, a very old olive tree has grown up over the grave of a wise *muezzin*. It is customary to write a wish on a slip of paper, wrap it in an olive leaf and put it into the hollow trunk.

- 28B2
- Kaleiçi
- Daily 8.30–5
- Clock Tower
- None; reasonable access
- Free
- Kaleiçi (➤ 54–5)

Alanya

The first real documentation of Alanya comes in 197BC, when the settlement, then known as Coracesium, was besieged by Antiochus III of Syria. The following century, a pirate chief, Diodotus Tryphon, overthrew the Syrians and built the fortress. Eventually, the pirates' activities grew too outrageous to ignore, Pompey was dispatched by Rome to sort them out, and Coracesium joined the empire. During the Byzantine era, the city changed its name to Kalonoros ('beautiful mountain'), changing again in 1221 when it was ceded to Seljuk Sultan Alâeddin Keykubad I, who renamed it Alaiye (City of Ala), after himself. The city grew and flourished around his extraordinary citadel (➤ 16), its star only fading after it was captured by the Ottomans in 1471.

Today, Alanya is a pleasant rather than inspiring place, with several very distinct zones—a small old town within the outer walls of the citadel; a thriving tourist zone around the charming old harbour; a busy, modern city inland; and big, brash hotels stretching along the beaches east and west.

The 3km (2 mile) beach, west of town, is the city's own main beach; the 8km (5 mile) to the east are fronted by resort hotels. Both have grey-brown sand, but are otherwise good, clean and usually crowded. The best beach in the area, at İncekum, about 20km (12 miles) west, is lined with huge resorts, which offer a range of watersports and other activities. There is almost nothing of entertainment value outside the hotels.

28C2
135km (84 miles) east of Antalya
Choice of restaurants (£–£££)
Damlataş Mağarasi Yanı, Damlataş Cad 1
0242 513 1240
Dolmuş stop on the seafront opposite Damlataş Cave
Few; reasonable access
Anamur (➤ 22), Alarahan (➤ 61), Side (➤ 68)

Above: *Modern Alanya curls around a sweeping bay*

Below: *Alanya's busy beach*

A Walk Around Alanya

Distance
About 7km (4 miles)

Time
Allow 2 hours

Start point
Beside the entrance to the İç Kale
28C2
Dolmuş or taxi

End point
Beside Damlataş Cave
28C2
Dolmuş or taxi

Lunch
At any of several harbour-front cafés; there are also plenty of drinks stops *en route* (£)

Most of this walk from the İç Kale (➤ 16) is down a steep hill, accessible to all of average fitness but hard on the knees. Anyone who tires *en route* can simply stop and flag down the next *dolmuş* or taxi.

Follow the hairpin bends of the main road down, keeping to the side (there are no pavements and you will be invisible to cars).

After about 1.5km (1 mile) a fork to the right leads to a viewing point over the harbour below.

After another 1km (half a mile), a path on the left leads to the ruins of the ancient city.

Meander around the narrow alleys before taking one of three routes back to the main road. Look for the city entrance arch; two old mosques: the Akşebe Türbesi (1230), containing the tomb of its founder, Akşebe Sultan, and the Süleymaniye Mosque (1231), reconstructed in the 16th century during the reign of Süleyman the Magnificent; and the 13th-century caravansarai, now the Bedesten Hotel.

Pizza on the pavement in holiday Alanya

After another 1.5km (1 mile), at the edge of the modern town, choose one of the narrow streets heading downhill on the harbour side; you will eventually come out near the Kızıl Kule (➤ 59). Walk around the harbour to the main street of cafés opposite the tour boats, then turn left and walk through the modern town along flat, easy Damlataş Street, or along the smaller Sultan Alâeddin Street, both of which come out next to the museum and tourist office.

What to See in Alanya

ALANYA MÜZESİ (ALANYA MUSEUM) ✪✪

There are only two display rooms in this well-presented little museum. The first covers the history of the region, with a broad range of exhibits including Hittite sculpture, Bronze Age pottery, coins from early Coracesium, Greek and Roman statues, and glass. The second room is the ethnographic section with carpets, costumes, gold and silver jewellery, and a reconstructed Turkish living room. The garden has a variety of mainly Roman sculptures, urns, sarcophagi and some farm implements.

28C2
Hilmi Baki Sokak, Damlataş Caddesi
0242 513 1228/7116
Tue–Sun, 9–12, 1.30–6.30
Moderate
Dolmuş stop on the seafront opposite Damlataş Cave
None; access reasonable

DAMLATAŞ MAĞARASI (WEEPING CAVE) ✪

This small seaside cave complex has two accessible chambers, both surrounded by wonderful curtains of strangely formed stalactites and stalagmites. The air is warm, thick and humid: 90–100 per cent humidity, at a constant temperature of 22–23°C (72–73°F), with high levels of carbon dioxide, natural ionization and radiation. Sufferers of asthma and rheumatism come here for a cure, which involves sitting in the cave for four hours a day for 21 days: it's said to have an 80 per cent success rate.

28C2
South end of western beach
Daily. For spa patients 6–10am. For general public 10–7
Inexpensive
Dolmuş stop on the seafront opposite Damlataş Cave
None; no access

İÇ KALE (INNER CITADEL, ➤ 16, TOP TEN)

KIZIL KULE (RED TOWER) ✪✪✪

This formidable 35m (115ft) octagonal tower was designed in 1226 by a Syrian architect for Sultan Alâeddin Keykubad I as the first line of defence of the Alanya dockyard and citadel (➤ 16). With its thick, red-brick walls, arrow slits and troughs for pouring boiling water, tar or oil on to attackers, it follows classical medieval castle design. Inside, each of the five storeys has eight sections of arched galleries surrounding a vast water cistern.

Fully restored in 1951, the tower now contains a small ethnographic museum with attractive displays of carpets and costumes, a few carved wooden panels and wonderful views from the battlements. The steps are extremely steep and unprotected in places so be very careful when making the ascent.

28C2
Eastern harbour
Daily 10–8
None

Kızıl Kule guards the fishing boats in Alanya harbour

Alanya Harbour Boat Trip

Alanya harbour is lined with *gülets*, all competing to take you on a trip around the harbour or along the coast.

The boat pulls away, giving an excellent view of the city and Kızıl Kule (➤ 59). It heads out past a series of five huge open workshops with arched roofs.

These are the Tersane, the last remaining Seljuk dockyard in Turkey, built by Sultan Alâeddin Keykubad I in about 1226 to service his navy. Continuing round the point, the Tophane Kule (Arsenal Tower) was built for defence, also in the 13th century, but was used as a cannon foundry in Ottoman times.

The boat passes under the citadel and cliff.

Alanya harbour is still used by jazzy local fishing boats

The most dramatic feature of the harbour tour is this magnificent red cliff, topped by the even more imposing curtain wall of the citadel (➤ 16): this is one of the best ways of experiencing its true size. A small opening in the cliff-face marks the bottom of an escape tunnel, leading right up into the castle. Further on, the agile (and thin) may be offered the chance to leap into a tiny tunnel leading right through the peninsula, then make the nerve-wracking jump back on to a wildly rocking boat.

Longer trips also involve stops at a series of sea caves.

These intriguing places include the shining Fosforlu (Phosphorus Cave), the Aşıklar Mağarası (Lovers' Cave), where a couple supposedly survived for three months in 1965, the Korsanlar Mağarası (Pirates' Cave), and Cleopatra's Beach, where legend says the great queen used to swim with Mark Anthony.

Time
Allow 1 or 2 hours (recommended) for harbour tours; there are also half and full-day trips

Start/end points
Alanya harbour
 28C2

Lunch
Usually provided for day trips; soft drinks on shorter trips.

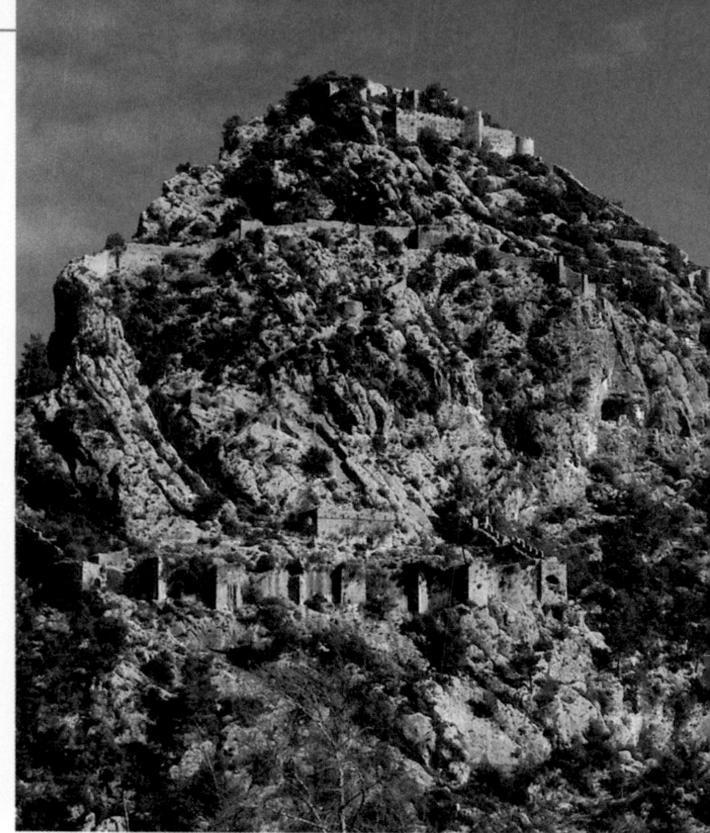

What to See in Pamphylia

ALARAHAN ✪✪

Set in a charming valley, next to a tumbling river, the well-preserved caravansarai at Alarahan was built in about 1231 by Seljuk Sultan Alâeddin Keykubad I. This one would have been used on the trading route between Konya and the port of Alanya. The caravanserais were built to a definitive architectural style that allowed separate areas for sleeping, storing goods and tending pack animals. There was usually a mosque and often a *hamam* and one central door for security purposes. Seljuks built more than 100 caravanserais in Anatolia, but it was the Ottomans who later refined the art to stimulate trade and raise revenue. Muslim pilgrims travelling to Mecca also used the caravanserais.

High on the mountain above is a dramatic fortress. No one knows its true origin and access involves a serious climb. Behind it is a rare painted bath house. Whitewater rafting has become a popular sport here.

- 28C2
- 38km (24 miles) west of Alanya; turn off the N-400 after 30km (19 miles)
- Open access
- Restaurants opposite (£)
- *Dolmuş*
- None, but some access to the caravansarai
- Free
- Alanya (➤ 57–60), Manavgat (➤ 67), Side (➤ 68)

Above: *The Seljuk Alara fortress was built to protect the mountain passes*

ASPENDOS (➤ 18, TOP TEN)

28C2
About 38km (24 miles) east of Antalya, off the N-400; turn off after 31km (19 miles)
Choice of restaurants in Aspendos (££)
Dolmuş to turn off
None
See Aspendos (➤ 18)

BELEK

Belek was developed by the Tourism Ministry in the early 1990s as a purpose-built environmental and golf tourism project. It's a seriously chic resort, with the sea to the south, man-made lakes, beautiful landscaping and four championship year-round golf courses. The local hotels are all luxurious, offering every imaginable activity and convenience. World-class athletes sometimes come here to train and relax away from the celebrity spotlight.

Did you know ?

The loggerhead turtle, Caretta caretta, *nests on 17 beaches in Turkey. Each year, between May and October, the turtles return to their home beach to breed. Born in darkness, the babies have to make a perilous 15-minute dash for the safety of the water. Beach umbrellas can crush the nests, while a light at night can disorientate the infants and send them in the wrong direction.*

28B2
90km (56 miles) north of Antalya, on the N-650
Burç Mah, Cumhuriyet Meydanı, Kültür Sarayı, Kat 2
Museum: Tue–Sun 9.30–12, 1.30–5.30
Museum: inexpensive

BURDUR

Due north of Antalya, across the Taurus Mountains, is an area of interesting natural lakes. Burdur Gölü is a shallow saltwater lake of reeds and alluvial land that provides an ideal habitat for the endangered white-headed duck. There are several fine beaches, including the 5km (3mile) Çendik Beach (2km/1 mile from town). Burdur town, on the eastern shore, has a 14th-century mosque, the Ulu Cami, and a small museum in the Ottoman Bulgurlu Medrese, containing many finds from Kremna (➤ 66) and Hacılar, an archaeological site dating back to the 6th millennium BC.

Belek National Golf Club

DÜDEN ŞELÂLESİ (DÜDEN FALLS)

The area around Antalya is limestone country, whose remote hills are littered with karst springs, sinkholes, underground rivers and waterfalls. Born of an underground river, the Düden Falls are a powerful and beautiful series of cascades crashing through a narrow gorge. The Upper Falls are a popular local picnic spot, with steps leading down to a soggy but very pretty walkway behind the curtain of water. The 20m (66ft) Lower Düden Falls gush straight over the cliff into the sea, and are best seen from a boat, which can tuck right in under the spray in a whirl of rainbows.

28B2
Upper Falls, Kızılırmak Caddesi, off the northern by-pass,14km (9miles) northeast of Antalya; Lower Falls about 10km (6 miles) east of Antalya, near Lara Beach
Open access
Cafés and restaurants near the Upper Falls (££)
None Free
Antalya (➤ 53–6)

EĞİRDİR

Built on the loveliest of the Pisidian lakes (and the second largest freshwater lake in Turkey), Eğirdir is a charming small town ringed by mountains. It was founded by Hittites, and has been a tourist resort since the 5th century BC, a popular stopover on the King's Way, between Ephesus and Babylon. In the Middle Ages, it became the local capital of the Hamidoğlu dynasty, and still has a rich, atmospheric collection of old Greek and Ottoman houses linked by a causeway. Springtime is the best time to see the flowers in bloom and the many migratory birds who stop here. There are a few Seljuk buildings, an excellent Thursday market and several good beaches near by, the best at Bedre Köyü, 8km (5 miles) out of town on the Barla road. Eğirdir is the starting point for the St. Paul Trail, Turkey's second long-distance walk. Nearby Davraz is a ski centre in winter.

28B2
86km (53 miles) northeast of Burdur via the N-685 and N-330
2 Sahil Yolu 13
0246 311 4388
Choice of *pansiyons* and restaurants on the islands and waterfront (££)
Dolmuş
None

Above: *The lower Düden Falls plunge straight into the sea*

İNCEKUM (ALANYA, ➤ 57)

İNCEKUM (ALANYA, ➤ 57)

KOCAİN MAĞARASI (KOCAIN CAVE) ✪

28B2
50km (31 miles) north of Antalya; take the Burdur road for 27km (17 miles), then turn off and continue to the village of Ahırtaş, from where there is a 2-hour walk up to the cave
Open access
Dolmuş to Ahırtaş
None
Free

This is the largest cave in Turkey, discovered in 1919 by an Italian caver, Guiseppe Moretti. It has an entrance 18m (59ft) high and 74m (242ft) across, leading into a cavern 633m (2,076ft) deep and 35m (115ft) high. Inside, immediately to the right of the entrance, is an altar; to the left are some Greek inscriptions. These, together with a huge water cistern, suggest that the cave was used as a church by early Christians. Further in, there are huge pillar stalactites, 8m (26ft) in diameter and 35m (115ft) long. Take a powerful torch, good boots and some drinking water.

KÖPRÜLÜ KANYON/SELGE ✪✪✪

28C2
About 99km (61 miles) east of Antalya; turn off the N-400 about 47km (29 miles) east of Antalya (just past Aspendos), 28km (17 miles) west of Side
Open access
Numerous restaurants along the river (£)
Dolmuş
None
Canyon free; Selge inexpensive (if the guard is there)
Antalya (➤ 17 and 53–6), Aspendos (➤ 18), Perge (➤ 24–5), Kurşunlu Şelâlesi (➤ 67), Side (➤ 68), Sillyon (➤ 69)

The prosaically named 'Canyon with a Bridge' is one of the most enchanting stretches of country in Pamphylia. Allow plenty of time for a leisurely meal of freshly tickled trout, a long country walk and the old stones at Selge.

From the turn-off, a good road winds up through the forested foothills into the Taurus Mountains, the air cooling noticeably as you reach a height of about 1,000m (3,280ft); much of the way, the road follows the Köprü Irmağı Valley. At the end of the tarmac road (43km/27 miles) is a cluster of restaurants and the base camp of many whitewater rafting companies. A short distance up the hill, take the left-hand fork of the gravel road, which crosses a beautiful single-arched Roman stone bridge, high above the gorge. Park just beyond this and walk down to the left for about 1km (half a mile), along the rim of the canyon, to a second Roman bridge. Follow the road to the right, as it heads up higher still, climbing 700m (2,296ft) on to the plateau and after 14km (9 miles) reaching the village of Altınkaya (Zerk) and the ruins of ancient Selge, once a Pisidian city of well over 20,000 people.

Although the road deteriorates and is precipitous in places, it is still driveable with care, and there are fabulous views across the wild valleys. As you get near, look out for the 'fairy chimneys', extraordinary wind-carved columns of soft volcanic ash.

The path leads through the modern village, which is totally entangled with the ancient city, whose marble columns double as fence posts and garden furniture. It brings you out at the back of a magnificent Greek-style theatre set against a backdrop of snow-capped mountains. From here, a path leads along the Roman main street to the *agora* and a Byzantine basilica. Beyond this are the remains of twin temples to Artemis and Zeus.

Opposite: *Köprülü Kanyon, a major excavation by a small but determined river*

28B2
About 115km (71 miles) north of Antalya, off the N650: 5km (3 miles) before Buçak, turn right through Çamlık to Kremna (8km/5 miles)
Open access
Dolmuş
None
Inexpensive (if guard is there)

KREMNA

The recently excavated Pisidian city of Kremna stands in a spectacular location on a clifftop promontory overlooking the Aksu River. It seems to have been one of the more modern cities in the region, but was certainly flourishing by the 5th century BC. From the late 1st century BC, it came under the direct control of the Roman Empire, and its defensive walls were built. Over a century later, under Hadrian, came a major rebuilding which gave it a grand 230m (251yds) colonnaded street, forum, monumental staircase, propylon, bath house and theatre.

More interesting, perhaps, are the remains of war. In AD270, the city was seized by a local brigand, Lydius, and the Romans had to wage a prolonged siege to get their city back. Archaeologists have found not only various weapons, including artillery, missiles and huge stones for rolling on to the enemy, but the remains of a siege mound (a ramp built under the walls by the Romans). Finds are in Burdur Museum (➤ 62).

KURŞUNLU ŞELÂLESİ (KURŞUNLU FALLS)

This is a pleasant, brief stop with high waterfalls plunging into a bubbling pool, surrounded by wooded cliffs and a small, very organized national park. Outside, there are decorative camels for expensive rides and exorbitant pictures, a huge car park and souvenir stalls. Inside, the cool, shady park has a children's playground, picnic tables and carefully marked walks to the falls and along the river.

- 28B2
- 23km (14 miles) east of Antalya, 7km (4 miles) off main road
- Daily 8.30–5.30
- Drink and snack stands (£)
- *Dolmuş*
- Moderate, parking fee

MANAVGAT

Manavgat is much larger and busier than neighbouring Side (➤ 68), but has little to hold the attention other than boat trips upstream to the Manavgat Şelalesi, an attractive waterfall 3km (2 miles) north of the town, surrounded by pleasant gardens, a good restaurant and several souvenir shops. The remote and virtually unknown ancient city of Seleukeia, with the remains of its city gate, bath, *agora*, market hall and temple, is an hour's mountain hike away.

- 28C2
- 5km (3 miles) east of Side
- Open access
- Restaurants in Manavgat (££); take refreshments if walking to Seleukeia
- *Dolmuş*
- None; Free
- Side (➤ 68)

PERGE (➤ 24, TOP TEN)

SAGALASSOS

Built on the steep slope of 2,000m (6,560ft) Mount Akdağ, about 1,500m (4,920ft) above sea level, dramatic Sagalassos was an important Pisidian frontier city from the 3rd millennium BC. Captured by Alexander, it became Roman, but always retained independence. There is an upper and a lower town, along with catacombs on the rock faces. Ruins from the Hellenistic period include a *heroön* (heroic shrine), decorated with a frieze of dancers (now in the village), a Doric temple, as well as a nymphaeum, *bouleterion* (council hall) and a potters' quarter. The Roman remains are far more extensive and include an *agora*, odeon, baths, a theatre, and a temple. The site has undergone comprehensive restoration.

- 28B2
- About 25km (16 miles) east of Burdur, off the N-685 to Isparta, through the village of Ağlasun
- None
- Moderate

The Manavgat Falls are a popular picnic place for local Turks escaping the searing summer heat

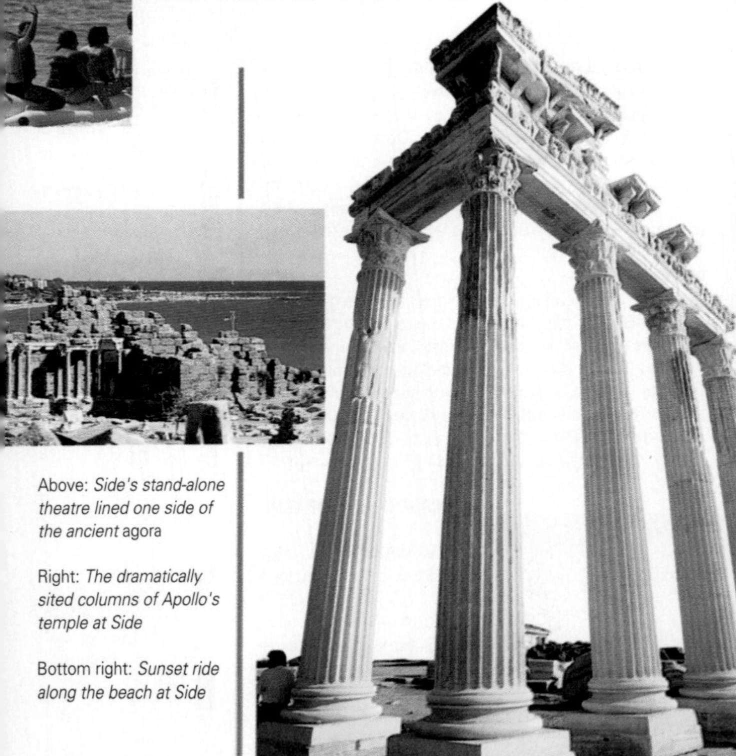

Above: *Side's stand-alone theatre lined one side of the ancient* agora

Right: *The dramatically sited columns of Apollo's temple at Side*

Bottom right: *Sunset ride along the beach at Side*

28C2
72km (45 miles) east of Antalya; turn off the N-400 3km (2 miles) west of Manavgat
Choice of restaurants (£–£££)
Dolmuş
Side Yolu Üzeri; off the main road, about 1km (half a mile) north of the town centre
0242-753 1265
None
Antalya (➤ 17, 53–6), Aspendos (➤ 18), Perge (➤ 24), Köprülü Kanyon (➤ 64), Kurşunlu Şelâlesi (➤ 67), Sillyon (➤ 69)

SİDE

Side is a pretty little town, built on a peninsula lined with long, gold sand beaches, with attractive old houses, waterfront restaurants and a harbour filled with sleek yachts. Even better, the modern town is built among the ruins of the ancient city, so sightseeing involves only a gentle stroll. In winter, it is idyllic. But Side has been a victim of its own success, suffering from rampant tourist development. In recent years, the town has settled down to 'middle age' and is now more sedate, better organized and neater, but it still has plenty of bars and late-night spots for those who want to prolong the evening.

Ancient Side ('pomegranate' in Anatolian) was founded in the 7th century BC and, courtesy of a roaring trade in slaves, sharp practice and piracy, grew into the richest port on the Pamphylian coast. The commercial harbour was the hub of a network that linked southern Anatolia with Syria, Egypt and Cyprus, trading wine, spices, oils, marble, dyes for textiles, and glass. It was torched by Arab invaders in the 10th century AD and abandoned after an earthquake in about 1150. Seljuks later restored it.

The approach road passes through the Hellenistic city gate, where long stretches of the city walls and aqueduct are visible. A few hundred metres on, the theatre dates from the 2nd century AD and was the largest in Pamphylia, with seating for 17,000 spectators. It stands on its own, partly supported by arches, not built into the hillside, as was more common. Next to it are the *agora* (probably the site of the slave market) and the semicircular remains of a 24-seat public lavatory. Beyond this, a path leads to a second *agora*, a Byzantine basilica and an episcopal palace, and over the dunes and city wall to the beach. On the opposite side of the road, the 5th-century AD bath house is now home to a fine **museum**. The main road passes through a 4th-century AD monumental arch, beside which stands an elaborate nymphaeum (fountain) honouring emperors Titus and Vespasian. It then follows the course of the old Roman road to the harbour. On the headland to the left, a few elegantly placed columns are all that remain of the once glorious temples of Apollo and Athena.

Museum and Archaeological Site

- On the main road at the entrance to the town
- 0242-753 1006
- Museum: Tue–Sun 9–12, 1.30–6.30. Archaeological site: open access; theatre currently closed for restoration
- Museum: inexpensive; archaeological site: free
- Paid car park for museum and archaeological site further up the hill, through the arch

SİLLYON

Sillyon's 200m (656ft), flat-topped acropolis is a landmark. Founded in around 1200BC, this was a thriving city long before Alexander tried—and failed—to capture it in 333BC. It continued to flourish throughout the Roman era.

The lower path passes the stadium, Hellenistic lower gate and gymnasium, later used as a Byzantine bishops' palace. From here, a heavily buttressed ramp leads past the necropolis to the Upper Gate. Within the walls are many Hellenistic structures, including several large public buildings, private houses, an odeon, a temple, numerous large and dangerously unmarked water cisterns and the remnants of a theatre. Nearly half the ruins were scattered across the plain below during a massive landslide in 1969.

- 28B2
- 33km (20 miles) east of Antalya. Turn off the N-400 after 25km (16 miles) and follow the side road for 8km (5 miles) to Asar Köyü; then steep climb
- Open access; None
- Free; use of a local guide recommended
- Antalya (➤ 17 and 53–6), Aspendos (➤ 18), Perge (➤ 24), Köprülü Kanyon (➤ 64), Kurşunlu Şelâlesi (➤ 67), Side (➤ 68)

In the Know

If you only have a short time to visit the Turkish Coast, or would like to get a real flavour of the region, here are some ideas:

Ways to Be a Local

Shake hands and spend a few minutes making small talk before getting down to business.
Learn a few words of Turkish; your efforts will be greatly appreciated.
Take off your shoes on entering a mosque or private house.
Accept a second glass of tea if offered; to refuse implies that the first was below standard.
Women should cover their heads, and both sexes should cover shoulders and knees when entering a mosque (don't enter at all during prayer times).
Lift your head backwards to say no, nod down for yes, shake it from side to side if you don't understand.
Do not point your finger, kiss or hug anyone of the opposite sex or blow your nose in public.
Never lose your temper or shout at anyone; to lose control is to lose respect.
Turks are patriotic; don't be rude about or make fun of Turkey, Islam, the Army or Atatürk.
Staring, standing close and touching you when talking is normal behaviour.

Good Places to Have Lunch

- Eat fish you caught that morning at a beach barbecue on Kekova Island (➤ 38).
- Relax on a sunny harbourfront terrace overlooking the fishing boats in Side (➤ 68).
- Eat freshly caught trout beside a mountain river at Saklıkent (➤ 47) or Köprülü Kanyon (➤ 64).
- Attack the buffet on a gently rocking *gület* after spending an hour snorkelling in turquoise waters.
- Picnic on the beach, under a shady pine tree, propped against a Lycian harbour wall at Phaselis (➤ 26).
- Unwind at a roadside restaurant on the Anamur–Silifke road, its terrace jutting dizzyingly over the the cliff (➤ 71, 10 Great Roads).
- Have a *döner kebab* and a glass of *ayran* in a simple backstreet café, surrounded by Turkish men chain-smoking black tobacco.
- Picnic on a mountain top overlooking the sea and

A fine Turkish carpet is a work of art and an heirloom of the future

terraced valleys at St. Simeon's Monastery (➤ 90).

- Share a *gözleme* (Turkish pancake) with the village women as they prepare the evening meal.
- Splurge at one of the elegant battlement restaurants in Antalya old town (➤ 54–55).

10 Top Activities

- Diving
- Four by four jeep safaris
- Golf
- Rafting, canoeing and kayaking
- Riding
- Sailing
- Skiing
- Trekking and abseiling
- Water-skiing, windsurfing and other watersports

10 Top Beaches

- Alanya (➤ 57)
- Belek, near Aspendos (➤ 62)
- Göynük, near Kemer (➤ 39)
- İncekum, near Alanya (➤ 57)
- İstuzu, near Dalyan (➤ 34)
- Marmaris (➤ 42)
- Ölüdeniz, near Fethiye (➤ 43)
- Patara (➤ 23)
- Phaselis (➤ 26)
- Side (➤ 68)

10 Great Roads

These are all chosen for their magnificent scenery. The driving is therefore extremely difficult; be very cautious.

Right: *Local women roll out dough for* gözleme

- 11km (7-mile) loop round the peninsula in Kaş.
- 90km (56-mile) drive from Kaş to Gömbe to the foothills of Mount Akdağ.
- 66km (41-mile) mountain road from Finike to Elmalı.
- 52km (32-mile) plains road between Elmalı and Korkuteli.
- 8km (5-mile) road through the woods to Çıralı and the Chimaera.
- Dramatic 75km (47-mile) stretch from Gazipaşa to Anamur, with 1,000m (3,280ft) cliffs.

Water slides and plenty of sun-worshippers at an Antalya waterpark

- Towering seacliff road from Anamur to Silifke (about 50km/31 miles of a 143km/89 mile journey).
- 49km (30-mile) main highway south from İskenderun to Antakya.
- Rough 20km (12-mile) round trip up to St. Simeon's monastery, near Antakya.
- 57km (35-mile) stretch from the main road to Köprülü Kanyon and Selge.

Cilicia and the Hatay

Most of the landscape in this easternmost section of the Turkish coast is less than inspiring: a broad plain with heavily industrialized cities such as Adana and İskenderun. But the area around Antakya is attractive, and the coast between Alanya and Silifke is spectacular.

Cilicia (roughly Alanya to Adana) was once part of the great Hittite Empire: many ancient settlements, such as Tarsus, are still thriving. There are hundreds of castles here, most dating back to the 9th to 13th centuries, when the area broke from the Byzantine Empire as the independent kingdom of Armenia. Beyond Cilicia, the Hatay is a finger of land pointing down to the Syrian border, ceded to Turkey by France in 1939. There is a greater sense of Asia here and the area has few foreign tourists—you are now definitely in the East!

‘Antioch is like the pantaloon whose clothes are far too wide for his lean shanks; the castle walls go climbing over rock and hill, enclosing an area from which the town has shrunk.’

GERTRUDE BELL,
The Desert and the Sown (1907)

St. Peter's Church, Antakya—official founding place of the Christian Church

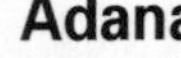

Adana

- 29F2
- 445km (276 miles) east of Alanya, on the N-400
- Atatürk Caddesi 13
  - 0322 363 1448
- Choice of restaurants (££)
- 5km (3 miles) west of town: *dolmuş* to centre
- North of centre, near top of Ziya Paşa Caddesi
- Karatepe (➤ 20), Mersin and Misis (➤ 84–5), Tarsus (➤ 90), Topprakale (➤ 91), Yılankalesi (➤ 92)

Although virtually unknown to tourists, Adana is the fourth largest city in Turkey (after Istanbul, Ankara and İzmir), with a population of over two million. There has been a settlement here since the Hittite era, when it may have been Danunas, capital of King Asitawatas, who also built Karatepe (➤ 20). Like all the surrounding cities, it is a centre of trade and commerce and has been a political football, overrun by a new invader almost every century, including the Arabs, Seljuks, Armenians and Mamelukes, until the Ottomans took over in 1516. In 1833, Egypt's Ibrahim Paşa, eager to throw off the Ottoman yoke, stationed troops in Adana.

Until the 20th century, Adana remained relatively insignificant, French colonists left the city in 1920. Since the arrival of the railway, however, it has far outstripped its neighbours and is now the regional capital and a wealthy, vibrant university city, surrounded by heavy industry and fertile agricultural Gukurara plains producing citrus, cotton and corn. It scarcely seems to miss the US troops with whom, until recently, the Turlks shared a massive airbase at neaby Incirlik. Its only must-see sight is the New Mosque. All the other sights are within walking distance of it.

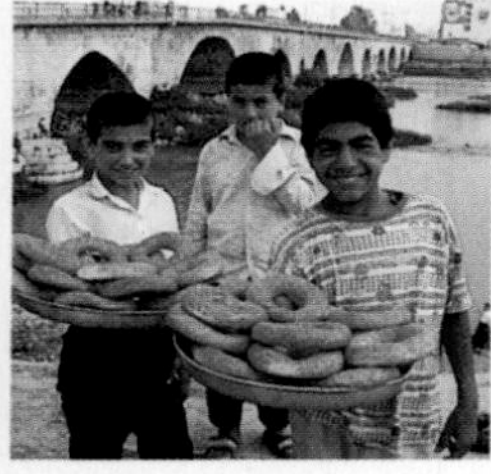

What to See in Adana

- Fuzuli Sokak (near the Sabancı Mosque)
- 0322 454 3855
- Tue–Sun 8.30–12, 1.30–5.30
- None
- Inexpensive

ARKEOLOJİ MÜZESİ (ARCHAEOLOGICAL MUSEUM) ✪

There are some nice exhibits in this neglected museum, including classical and Hittite statuary, mosaics, bronzeware, jewellery, coins and early pottery. Look for the marble sarcophagus and the crystal figure of a Hittite Storn God and try to ignore the general apathy.

- İnönü Caddesi
- 0322 363 3717
- Tue–Sun 8.30–12, 1.30–5
- None
- Inexpensive

ETNOGRAFYA MÜZESI (ETHNOGRAPHY MUSEUM) ✪

Housed in a Byzantine church, this is a small but well-thought-out collection, with a variety of musical instruments, household objects, jewellery, carpets and *kilims*, traditional embroidery, illustrated manuscripts and a reconstruction nomads' tent.

- Fuzuli Caddesi, next to the river
- None
- Free, but donations appreciated
- Open during daylight hours

SABANCI MERKEZ CAMİ (CENTRAL MOSQUE) ✪✪✪

With a dome 54m (177ft) high and space for 30,000 people, this magnificent mosque (begun in 1988) is the largest in Turkey and the only one in the country, other than Istanbul's Blue Mosque, to be allowed six minarets. Outside, dome is elegantly heaped on dome in a fashion similar to the Selimiye Mosque in Edırne, its shining white marble reflected in the river. The interior, using a mix of decorative tiles and Koranic calligraphy, liberally sprinkled with gold leaf, is based on—and every bit as spectacular as—the Blue Mosque. Its benefactors, the Sabancıs, are locals and among Turkey's best-known industrial families.

From here it is a pleasant walk along the Seyhan River to the 310m (1,017ft), multi-arched Taş Köprü (Stone Bridge), built by Emperor Hadrian (AD 117–38), and restored by Justinian, the Ottomans and various others.

Left: *Selling* simit *(bread rings) by the old bridge, Adana*

ULU CAMİ (GREAT MOSQUE) ✪✪

The very different but equally beautiful Ulu Cami was built in 1541 as a legacy from Halil Bey, a member of the ruling Ramazanoğlu family, who died in 1507 and is buried here. It was enlarged in 1541. The mosque's Syrian design has black and white marble stripes around the the distinctive eight-cornered minaret, and black, white and yellow İznik tiles round the entrance and *mihrab*.

Opposite is an active *medrese* (religious school), built at the same time. Nearby are two other historic mosques: the Akça Mesçit and the Ramazanoğlu Camii, both built in the early 15th century, also in the Syrian style.

To the left, off Abidin Paşa Caddesi, in the old town
Daily 8.30–5
None
Free

The Merkez Cami is an impressive sight beyond the Taş Köprü

A Drive from Adana to Cappadocia

Distance
About 310km (192 miles) one way, from Adana to Ürgüp

Time
Allow 3–4 hours driving time one way. It is possible to get a brief glimpse in one long day. Preferably allow 3 days

Start point
Adana
29F2

End point
Ürgüp
29E2

Weird stone chimneys turn the Cappadocia landscape into a fantasy world

A side trip to Cappadocia can only give you a short introduction to the extraordinary landscapes and the wealth of art and history in the area. Cappadocia is a triangle of land roughly bordered by Niğde, Nevşehir and Kayseri. Thirty million years ago, two volcanoes—Erciyes Dağ (3,916m/12,922ft) and Hasan Dağ (3,268m/10,719ft))—spewed soft lava (tuff), ash and mud over the local basalt plain. This has eroded unevenly, creating extraordinary columns and cones (known as 'fairy chimneys') in a dazzling array of colours from purple to yellow, russet and red. The tuff is soft until exposed to the air, making it easy for generations, from the Hittites onwards, to carve out at least 37 extraordinary underground cities, some housing up to 20,000 people. During the early Christian years, the area became a refuge from the Romans, and then from Arab invasions. The monks left a stunning legacy of around 3,000 rock churches. Those with the time can explore the area by horse, mountain-bike or hot-air balloon.

Leave Adana on the E-90 or N-400, heading west towards Tarsus (► 90). After 35km (22 miles), turn north on to the O-21 motorway or the N-750. The roads join after 64km (38 miles), at Pozantı. Continue for 46km (29 miles), then take the N-805 north to Niğde (53km/33 miles).

There are fine Seljuk and Mongol buildings and an 11th-century citadel in Niğde, but the must-see sight is Eski Gümüş (14km/9 miles north, off the Kayseri road), a rock-cut Byzantine monastery with superb frescoes and an open courtyard. Niğde makes Turkey's tasitest ewe's milk cheese, while Kayseri makes some of Turkey's finest carpets.

After 10km (6 miles), turn left on to the N-765. After 17km (11 miles), at Gölcük, turn left for the Ilhara Valley.

A path with 435 steps drops down into the 10km (6

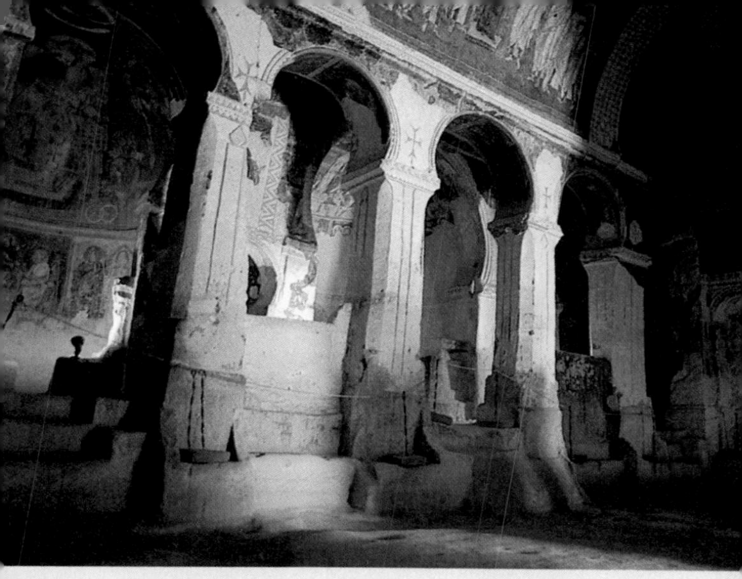

miles), 150-m (492-ft) deep gorge, carved by the Melendiz River. It is an extraordinary place, with an estimated 4,500 man-made caves and 105 churches and shrines surrounded by fabulous scenery rich in wildlife. Several of the churches have fine Byzantine frescoes and glory in descriptive names such as Direkli Kilise (Church with the Columns) and Kırk Damalı Kilise (Church with Forty Roofs).

Return to the main road and keep straight on for another 63km (39 miles) through Derinkuyu (17km/11 miles) and Kaymaklı (9km/6 miles) to Nevşehir.

The labyrinthine underground cities of Derinkuyu and Kaymaklı, created by carving tunnels between deep wells, are almost invisible from the surface. Linked by a 9km (6-mile) tunnel, they had constant temperature, humidity and good ventilation from air shafts. The top eight storeys (of a probable 20) are open at Derinkuyu; four at Kaymaklı.

Turn right along the N-767 for the Göreme Valley and Ürgüp (about 20km/12 miles).

In the 6th–11th centuries, the Göreme Valley, now a national park, **open-air museum** and UNESCO site, was Cappadocia's main centre of Christianity, with some magnificent Byzantine frescoes. The tour takes in seven painted churches, culminating in the fabulous Tokalı Kilise (Buckle Church). Avanos, north of Göreme, produces wonderful pottery. Ürgüp is an attractive town, with old Greek houses backing on to caves, and a thriving tourist centre with the region's main museum and small hotels.

The glorious interior of the Tokalı Kilise

Lunch/accommodation

Ataman Hotel/Restaurant
✉ Orta Mah, Uzundere Cad.,Göreme (£££)
☎ 0384 271 2310

Tourist Offices

Regional Directorate
✉ Atatürk Bulv, Devlet Hastanesi Önü, Nevşehir ☎ 0384 212 9573
✉ Kağnı Pazarı 61, Melihgazi, Kayseri ☎ 0352 222 3903
✉ Belediye Sarayı, C Blok, Kat: 3, Niğde ☎ 0388 232 3401
✉ Park İçi, Kayseri Caddesi, Ürgüp; next to the museum ☎ 0384 341 4059

Open-Air Museum

☎ 0384 271 2167

ANAMUR

29D1
128km (79 miles) east of Alanya; 223km (138 miles) west of Mersin on the N-400
Otogar Binası Kat 2
0324 814 3529
Some restaurants (£)
None
Silifke (➤ 86–7)

Museum
İskele Caddesi
0324 814 1677
Daily 8–5
Inexpensive

Built on a small plain between the Sultansuyu and Tatlısu rivers, surrounded by the Taurus Mountains and cut off from both Alanya to the west and Mersin to the east by many kilometres of treacherous but spectacular roads along the sea cliffs, Anamur is a rarity. Although the town itself is a drab little place about 5km (3 miles) inland, its seaside twin, İskele is a small, almost untouched seaside town whose few hotels are inexpensive. Most of the visitors are Turkish, but anyone willing to make the trek will find it very rewarding. Not only does it have one of Turkey's finest castles (Mamure Kalesi, ➤ 22), an excellent ancient city, and a small but interesting **museum**, it also has a good beach. Local wildlife includes loggerhead turtles and a small colony of monk seals.

Occupying the southernmost tip of Anatolia, 6km (4 miles) east, Anamurium (meaning 'windy cape') was established by the Hittites in around 1200BC, but first enters history with the invasion of the Assyrians in the 8th century BC. It became a bishopric in the early Byzantine era, but never really recovered from a devastating earthquake in AD580, closely followed by the first Arab invasions. The impressive ruins remaining today mainly date from the 2nd to 5th centuries AD. Highlights include a necropolis as large and well built as a town, some of its

Mosque inside the Crusader castle Mamure Kalesi in Anamur

Crusader castle of Mamure Kalesi, in Anamur

350 tombs boasting painted interiors; a bath and gymnasium; a basilica; a lighthouse; an odeon and a theatre. The bath and several private houses still have mosaic floors. There is a beach and picnic site at the far end, under a cliff with a few remnants of the citadel.

ANAVARZA (DİLEKKAYA) 

The lower city at this remote, entirely unexcavated site was almost entirely destroyed by an earthquake in Roman times and rebuilt by Emperor Justinian. It then changed hands many times until it became a minor capital of Armenia in 1100. It was abandoned in 1375. Visible remains include a number of mosaics, a stadium, an amphitheatre, a theatre, baths, a triumphal arch and tombs. It takes some serious scrambling to climb up the 200m (656ft) escarpment to the heavily defended citadel, built by the Armenians on top of much older fortifications.

- 29F2
- 72km (45 miles) northeast of Adana: left off N-400 at Ceyhan; then right towards Aysehoca
- None
- Free; use a local guide
- Karatepe (➤ 20), Misis (➤ 85), Topprakale (➤ 91), Yılankalesi (➤ 92)

29F1

191km (118 miles) southeast of Adana, via the N-400/ E-90 and N817/E-91

Choice of restaurants (£–£££)

Coaches from Adana and on to Syria; *dolmuş*

None

Çevlik, Harbiye (➤ 83), İskenderun (➤ 84), St Simeon's Monastery (➤ 90)

Sen Piyer Kilisesi

2km (1 mile) off Kurtuluş Caddesi, northeast of city centre

Tue–Sun 8–12, 1.30–6. Citadel, open access

ANTAKYA

In the Hatay, as everywhere else in Turkey, there was a power vacuum after the death of Alexander the Great in 324BC. Here, Seleukos Nikator I took control. In about 300BC, he chose as his capital the small town of Antigonus, on the Orontes River, in the foothills of Mount Silpius. This not only barred the classic invasion route, but also stood right on the Silk Road that crossed from China through the Middle East to Europe. Renamed Antioch after Seleukos' father, the city prospered, especially after it was ceded to Rome in 64BC. Within a century, it was the third largest city in the Roman Empire (after Rome and Alexandria), the capital of the Roman province of Syria, and famous as a centre of religion, learning, science and, of course, trade. Amenities included aqueducts, street-lighting and a colonnaded main street 6.5km (4 miles) long, as well as the usual theatre, stadium, baths and other civic buildings. With a cosmopolitan population, including a large Jewish community, it became one of the key centres of early Christianity.

Inevitably, life was not all easy. The Christians were ruthlessly persecuted. The city was nearly destroyed by two great fires, a massive outbreak of plague and several horrendous earthquakes, one of which was said to have killed 250,000 people. In 638, the city was conquered by the Muslim Persians. In 1084, it fell to the Seljuk Turks, and in 1098 it was besieged for nine months by the Crusaders, who set it up as a Christian principality under the Knights of St. John. It was captured by the Mamelukes (Egyptian rulers) in 1268, became part of the Ottoman Empire in 1516 and, with the collapse of the Silk Road, decayed into a sleepy backwater. It was a French protectorate from 1918 until 1939, when the Turkish Army moved in; a year later it voted to return to Turkey.

Modern Antakya is an attractive, friendly place, well off the beaten track, although it is a popular place of pilgrimage. The broad boulevards of the left bank contain some of the smartest shops in southern Turkey, in sharp contrast to the market stalls, kiosks and huddled old houses of the right bank old town. Antakya Archaeological Museum ➤ 19) is a world-class museum of Roman mosaics.

St. Peter lived in Antioch from AD47 to 54, holding secret gatherings of converts in the **Sen Piyer Kilisesi** (St. Peter's Cave), just outside the city, and this is commonly regarded as the very first Christian church. It was here that Peter, Paul and Barnabas decided to call their religion 'Christian' (Acts 11:26), and it went on to become the seat of a powerful patriarch. In 1963 it was recognized by the Roman Catholics as the world's first cathedral, marked at a special service here on 29 June each year.The arched entrance built by the Crusaders in the 11th century was prettied up in 1863. Inside, the simple church has a plain

stone altar, in front of which are remnants of a 5th-century AD mosaic floor. To the right is a spring, said to spout holy water; to the left an escape tunnel (blocked). A winding 15km (9-mile) road leads on up to the ruined citadel, rebuilt from the 4th century BC to the 10th century AD.

St. Peter's Church, a simple cave just outside ancient Antioch

A Walk Around Antakya

Distance
About 2km (1 mile)

Time
Allow 1–2 hours

Start point
Beside the Archaeological Museum, on the city centre roundabout beside the Rana Köprüsü (Old Bridge)
29F1
Dolmuş or taxi

End point
Rana Köprüsü
29F1
Dolmuş or taxi

Lunch
Anadolu (££)
Hurriyet Caddesi 50/C
0326 215 1541

Start at the Archaeological Museum.

The Asi (Orontes) River neatly divides Antakya in two. To the left, the pleasant 'new' town owes a great deal to French inter-war town planning. Note particularly the splendid art-deco cinema on Atatürk Caddesi, the French Assembly Buildings, set in beautiful gardens, and the Korean Methodist Church on Hükümet Caddesi, founded in 2000. More than 5,000 Turkish soldiers fought in the Korean War in 1953 and 1954, founding a school in Seoul before they left; the reciprocal spirit remains healthy.

Cross the river on the Rana Köprüsü (Old Bridge).

The bridge looks modern, but lurking under the metal and tar is a 3rd-century AD foundation. Straight on, the imposing minaret of the Ulu Cami marks the start of the old town.

Turn half right along Hürriyet Caddesi, one of the main streets of the old town.

Restaurants and shops selling künefe line this road, which curves up round some fine old houses to two elegant neo-classical mansions, part of the university.

From here, continue uphill and turn left along Salâhl;. Kuvvetler Caddesi, or, more interestingly, go back down and wind your way through the maze of pretty back streets.

In either case, you will eventually come out on Kurtuluş Caddesi, where rows of rundown mansions are boarded up.

The narrow, shady alleys at the heart of old Antakya are jammed with tiny shops and stalls

Walk along Kurtuluş Caddesi until you reach the Habib Neccar Camii.

This Ottoman mosque, with a 17th-century minaret, was built within the shell of a Byzantine church.

Turn left down the hill on Kemal Paşa Caddesi. About halfway down, the side alleys fill with the stalls of the main bazaar. Choose your own route, and you will end at the Rana Köprüsü.

ÇEVLİK ✪

Founded as his capital by the first Seleucid ruler, Seleukos Nikator I, in the 4th century BC, the ancient harbour of Seleucia ad Piera later served as Antioch's port. The tiny, modern village of Çevlik still has an attractive working harbour and a pleasant, if short stretch of beach. On the hill above, the Titus Tüneli is an impressive 7-m (23-ft) high storm drain, carved from the rock under emperors Titus and Vespasian to protect the harbour from the effects of floods and silt. The water is not recommended for swimming due to pollution from nearby İskenderun (➤ 84). Samandağ, though billed as a resort, is a most unattractive place and best avoided.

- 29F1
- Samandağ 25km (16 miles) west of Antakya; Çevlik 5km (3 miles) north of Samandağ
- Several restaurants along the seafront in Çevlik (£)
- Open access
- None
- Titus Tüneli: inexpensive
- St. Simeon's Monastery (➤ 90)

HARBİYE (DAPHNE) ✪

Ancient Daphne was a busy place. The nymph Daphne, hotly pursued by Apollo, prayed for delivery and was turned into a laurel bush. Apollo took a branch and wove himself a laurel wreath, which became the symbol of victory. It was also here that Cyparissus accidently shot his pet stag. Apollo turned the grieving man into a cypress tree, which became the symbol of mourning. Most contentiously, it was here that Paris was asked to judge a goddesses' beauty competition. He awarded the golden apple to Aphrodite, who promised him in return the loveliest woman in the world, Helen—who happened to be married to someone else. And that led to the Trojan War.

Daphne (now called Harbiye) was the summer resort of Roman Antioch, a wealthy suburb whose 2nd- to 4th-century villas revealed a treasure trove of mosaics (➤ 19). Anthony and Cleopatra were married here in 40BC. Today, the deep, green valley and a waterfall are overwhelmed by tatty souvenir stalls which sell lovely laurel (daphne) soap.

- 29F1
- 8km (5 miles) south of Antakya on the N-825
- None
- Free
- Antakya (➤ 19 and 80–2), Çevlik (➤ 83), St. Simeon's Monastery (➤ 90)

The richly adorned walls of the mosaics museum in Antakya

29F2
56km (35 miles) north of Antakya, on the N-825
Atatürk Bulv 49/B
0326 614 1620
Antakya (➤ 80–82)

Above: *Romantic and tragic, the Kiz Kalesi stands marooned on an islet 200m (656ft) offshore*

İSKENDERUN ✪

This busy commercial and industrial port was founded in 333BC by Alexander the Great, following his decisive victory against the Persians in the Battle of Issos. There are some surviving Armenian and Christian churches in the backstreets and the promenade still has some of its French colonical architecture. Above all, however, it is overwhelmed by industrial pollution. To the south, Belen lies on a mountain pass, the Gates of Syria, the main route into Turkey for the caravans of the Silk Road and invading armies. North of İskenderun, Yakacik (Payas), is the Sokulla Mehmet Pasa mosque and caravansarai complex, built by Sinan in 1574. Its strategic position turned Payas into a prosperous trading and border town. It was also on the pilgrim route to Mecca.

KARATEPE (➤ 20, TOP TEN)

29E1
25km (16 miles) east of Silifke
Daily 8.30–5
Several restaurants and cafés along the seafront overlooking Kiz Kalesi (££)
Dolmuş to Korykos; ask one of the boatmen at the beach motel next door to take you
None Free, except for the boat
Narlıkuyu (➤ 86), Silifke (➤ 86–7), Uzuncaburç (➤ 92)

KIZ KALESİ ✪✪

Two castles stare at each other across 200m (656ft) of sea. Offshore, perched on a tiny island only accessible by boat, is Kız Kalesi (Maiden's Castle), built in 1104 by Byzantine admiral, Eugenius during the early days of the Crusades. Its name derives from a local legend that a king, on hearing from an oracle that his beloved daughter would die of a snake bite, imprisoned her on the snake-free island. Unfortunately, a viper hid in a basket of fruit taken into the castle, and the prophecy was fulfilled.

Onshore, 12th-century Korykos Castle reuses the materials of earlier Greek and Roman fortifications. Various remains of the once-flourishing ancient city, mentioned by Herodotos in the 5th century BC, lie scattered across the headland. About 8km (5 miles) north, at Adam Kayalar, 1st- to 2nd-century AD Roman sculptures are cut into the cliff.

29E2
72km (45 miles) west of Adana on the N-400

MERSİN (IÇEL) ✪

Lying on the fertile Cilician plain, Mersin became a city only during the waning years of the Ottoman Empire, in about 1852. At this time, it was inhabited by Turks, Greeks and

Armenians. In the 1950s it was designated as a strategic trans-shipment point to service the productive floodplain of the Euphrates River. In fact, most investment bypassed Mersin in favour of an ambitious irrigation project, the GAP and located further east, to harness the Tigris and Euphrates rivers. It is now a city of 2 million people, with broad boulevards and greenery along the seafront. Its dockland culture gives it less appeal for tourists, except as a departure point for ferries to Northern Cyprus. It takes its name from the many myrtle (*mersin*) trees once found in the area. About 9km (6 miles) south, in a scruffy park in suburban Soğuksu, the extraordinary tumulus of Yümüktepe has revealed 23 layers of civilizations, dating from 6300BC to the 12th century AD. There is little to see here now; finds are on display in the museum.

Several restaurants in harbour area (££)
İsmet İnönü Bulv 5
0324 238 3271

Museum
Atatürk C Kültür Merkezi yanı
0324 231 9618
Tue–Sun 9–12, 1.30–4.30
None
Inexpensive

Plastic is big in Turkey

MİSİS (YAKAPINAR) ✪✪

This is a very unusual site. There is an ancient city, said to have been founded by Hittite King Mopsus, curled around the village gardens and sidestreets. However, Misis is even more interesting as a slice of Turkish rural life. The men play backgammon in the street; the children herd goats, and the women make bread for dinner. The much-heralded museum is simply one large Roman mosaic, said to represent Noah's Ark, covered and left *in situ*. Around the village you will also discover a Roman stone bridge, remnants of the city walls, an aqueduct, a temple, a theatre, an even more ancient tell (mound), an Ottoman caravansarai and a couple of mosques.

29F2
About 40km (25 miles) east of Adana, 3km (2 miles) off the N-400
Museum officially open daily 8.30–12, 1–4.30; in practice kept locked: local children will let you in
Cafés in the village (£)
None
Museum: inexpensive
Adana (➤ 74–75), Topprakale (➤ 91),

29E1
20km (12 miles) east of Silifke; the caves are 3km (2 miles) inland, both off the N-400
Daily 8:30–5
Several good fish restaurants line the waterfront (££); café next to the caves' car park (£)
Dolmuş
None Inexpensive

NARLIKUYU ✪

The coastal village of Narlıkuyu ('well of the pomegranate') was once a port with a famous bath complex, of which only the 4th-century AD floor mosaic, depicting the Three Graces, remains. Water from the spring that fed the complex (still bubbling today) was said to give wisdom to those who drank from it.

A short distance inland are the Corycian Caves, better known as Cennet ve Cehennem (Heaven and Hell), and regarded as sacred by pagans, Christians and Muslims. At the edge of the Cave of Heaven stands the temple of Zeus Corychios, which was used as the foundation of a 4th- to 5th-century Christian basilica (next to the car park).

To reach Heaven (Cennet Deresi), climb down 452 steps to the bottom of the larger chasm (200m/656ft long, 90m/295ft wide and 70m/230ft deep), where a small Byzantine chapel, dedicated to the Virgin, blocks the entrance of the Cave-Gorge of Hell.

Continue along a slippery path down the gorge for 200m (656ft), listening out for the intermittent roar of an underground river (thought by some to have been the Styx), to reach the cave entrance to Hades, the site of an oracle.

Above: *The Three Graces still decorate the long-abandoned bath-house at Narlıkuyu*

Right: *Silifke's massive fortress totally dominated the surrounding plains*

About 75m (246ft) north is a 120-m (394-ft) deep, sinkhole—the Cehennem (Pit of Hell), where Zeus imprisoned Typhon, the many-headed, fire-breathing serpent, who was father of Cerberus, guard dog of Hell. This can be reached only by experienced climbers.

Under the souvenir shop is a 200-m (656-ft) long cave system with beautiful stalactites and stalagmites, said to aid asthma sufferers. There are still some remains of a Byzantine town in the surrounding countryside.

29D1
217km (135 miles) east of Anamur; 161km (99 miles) west of Adana on the N-400
Gazi Mah, Veli Gürten Bozbey Cad 6
0324 714 1151
Kiz Kalesi (➤ 84), Narlıkuyu (➤ 86), Uzuncaburç (➤ 92)

SİLİFKE ✪✪

This small, busy market town, about 10km (6 miles) inland, was one of nine founded by and named after Alexander's egocentric general, Seleukos Nikator I, in the 3rd century BC. It stands on the Göksu Nehri (Sky Blue Water), in which Frederick Barbarossa drowned in 1190 (➤ 88), and is dominated by a magnificent **castle. First** built by the Byzantines in the 7th century as protection against the Arabs, the castle was heavily altered by the Armenians and Crusaders before reverting to Turkish hands in 1471.

From the battlements there is a splendid view over the whole town, which helps pinpoint the remains of ancient Seleukeia Tracheia. On the river, a modern stone bridge still sports Vespasian's inscription of AD78. Nearby, a park surrounds the acropolis fortified by the Assyrians in the 8th century BC: there are faint traces of a Roman theatre and the Seleucid fort. The temple of the famous Roman oracle of Apollo Sarpedonios is on İnönü Bulvarı. Other fragments include a stretch of aqueduct, a vast Byzantine water cistern, and the necropolis, all near the foot of the castle hill. The various finds are collected in the town **museum**.

About 1km (half a mile) west is the tiny 4th-century AD Byzantine cave church of Haghia Thekla, the hermitage of a 1st-century AD saint, St. Paul's first convert, who is said to have flown bodily up to heaven to escape martyrdom.

Just south of Silifke, the marshlands of the Göksu Delta are home to turtles and many species of bird.

Castle

- 4km (2.5 miles) from the town centre, turn off the main road at the western (Anamur) entrance to the town
- Daily 8.30–5
- Restaurant/café beside the car park (£)
- None
- Inexpensive

Museum

- Taşucu Yolu Üzeri (main Antalya road)
- 0324 714 1019
- Tue–Sun 8–12, 1.30–5
- Inexpensive

Mevlâna Tekke is a place of pilgrimage and the heart of the dervish monastic order

Distance
252km (156 miles)

Time
Allow 2–3 days for the round-trip, including sightseeing and side tracks. This excursion can be done in conjunction with the Cappadocia tour (➤ 76–7) by taking the N-300 via Aksaray to Nevşehir (207km/128 miles).

Start/end point
Silifke
 29D1

Lunch
Restaurants in Mut, Karaman, roadside cafés along the route; the best option is to take a picnic up to Binbir Kilise

Dinner
Horozlu Han Kervansaray (£££)
Restored medieval caravansaray, with floor shows on many evenings.
✉ Konya-Ankara Yolu Üzeri, TNP Yani, Konya
☎ 0332 248 3115

A Drive to Konya

This is one of the most beautiful roads in Turkey. The first half follows a winding mountain route; the second is a flat, straight drive across the plains.

Head north from Silifke on the N-715.

About 7km (4 miles) north of Silifke on the N-715, a memorial marks the spot where the Holy Roman Emperor, Frederick Barbarossa, drowned in 1190, in the Göksu River, while leading the Third Crusade. He was pickled in vinegar to preserve him for burial at St. Peter's Cathedral, Antioch (➤ 80) before being returned to Germany.

Continue along the main road for 76km (47 miles) to Mut.

The busy market town of Mut has a 14th-century mosque, Lal Aği Camii, a fortress and two domed tombs. About 20km (12 miles) north, the well-preserved Byzantine monastery of Alahan (2km/1 mile off the main road) overlooks the wild Göksu Gorge.

Return to the main road and head north for 73km (45 miles) to Karaman.

Between 1277 and 1467, Karaman became the centre of a powerful autonomous emirate. Several monuments date from the period, including the fortress, the mosque, Yunus Emre Camii, and several religious houses and schools—the Hatuniye Medresesi, the İbrahim Bey İmareti and the Ak Tekke. The museum holds fascinating finds from the 6th-millennium BC site of Canhasan, about 13km (8 miles) northeast. The valley of Binbir Kilesi (1,001 churches) is 38km (24 miles) north of town, near the village of Dinek (the last 8km/5 miles are up a rough but passable track). From the 5th to 6th and 9th to 14th centuries it was crammed with monasteries, many of which, including some with frescoes, survive in scattered ruins.

About 72km (45 miles) north of Karaman, Çatalhöyük (around 6500–5400 BC) is the second oldest known city in the world (after Jericho). It was the first place known to use irrigation, keep domestic animals and make carpets. There is little to see here now: the finds are all in Ankara's Museum of Anatolian Civilizations or in Konya.

Continue for a further 56km (35 miles) to Konya.

Konya is a large, modern city. Inhabited since Hittite times, it was capital of the Seljuk Sultanate of Rum from 1071 to 1308 and probably still has a good claim as the Islamic capital of Turkey; be aware of religious sensibilities. By far the most important sight is the **Mevlâna Tekke Müzesi.** This was the monastery of the 13th-century mystic philosopher and poet, Jalal ad-Din ar-Rumi, better known as Mevlâna, founder of the Sufi monastic order of dervishes, who worshipped God through music and dance. The building has been a museum since Atatürk abolished the order in 1925, but it is still a centre of pilgrimage, containing Mevlâna's tomb and, supposedly, hairs from the Prophet Mohammed's beard, along with a magnificent collection of musical instruments, ancient manuscripts and rare 13th-century *kilims*. Other museums in the city include the Seljuk Karatay Medresesi, containing a fine collection of ceramics; the archaeological museum and the Koyunoğlu Museum. There are also several beautiful mosques and religious institutions, of which the finest must be the 13th-century Seljuk Alâeddin Camii.

Return to Silifke along the same route.

Accommodation

Otel Selçuk (££)

Alâeddin Caddesi 4, Konya

0332 350 4290; fax: 0332 353 2529

Tourist Information

Mevlâna Cad 21, Konya

0332 351 1074

Festival of the Whirling Dervishes, 9–17 Dec (this annual pilgrimage is the only time the dervish order is 'in residence'; booking essential)

Mevlâna Tekke Müzesi

Mevlâna Meydanı

0332 351 1215

Summer: Mon 10–6, Tue–Sun 9–6; winter: Tue–Sun 9–5:30

Expensive

The drive north to Konya is a magnificent scenic treat; give yourself time to savour the surroundings

29F1
Turn off the Samandağ road 22km (14 miles) west of Antakya
Open access
None
Free
Çevlik (➤ 83), Antakya (➤ 80–82)

ST. SIMEON'S MONASTERY

One of the oddest of the early Christian zealots was St. Simeon Stylites the Younger, who sat on a pillar to commune with God. Starting on a humble rock, he eventually graduated to a 13m (43ft) column of stone on a high promontory overlooking the sea. There he remained for 25 years, chained to the pillar. A large monastery grew up around the column to cater for the many pilgrims who came to listen to his pronouncements; and he started a trend, with some 250 people eventually inhabiting columns across Syria. Today, the base of the column remains, surrounded by the ruined monastery. The views are magnificent.

Below: *Cleopatra's Gate, the entrance to ancient Tarsus*

29E2
38km (24 miles) west of Adana
Choice of cafés and restaurants (£–££)
None
Adana (➤ 74), Mersin (➤ 84)

Museum
Kulat Paşa Medrese, Tabakhane Mah, 155 Sokak, No 1
0324 613 0625
Tue–Sun, 8–5
None
Moderate

TARSUS

Legend says Tarsus was founded by Seth, son of Adam; archaeologists say the town has been here since about 300BC. It remained the most important city in the area until its lagoon silted up and cut it off from the sea. In 333BC Alexander the Great caught a chill swimming in the waterfall (the *şelale*) on the edge of town; in 41BC, Mark Anthony summoned Cleopatra here for punishment after she backed the wrong side in the Battle of Philippi. She arrived in glory and he fell in love. A few decades later, a local Jew named Saul became St. Paul (➤ 14).

Over the years Tarsus has been sacked by the Arabs, Seljuks, Crusaders, Armenians, Mamelukes and Ottomans. Little remains of its illustrious past, but the narrow streets of the old town still groan with age, while the wood and stone houses are typical of the Repubican 1920s.

At the city entrance is a Roman arch, known as the Kancık Kapışı (Bitch's Gate) or Cleopatra's Gate, although it has nothing to do with her. A few blocks away are two mosques: the Kilise Cami, a 14th-century Armenian church; and the Makam Camii, said to mark the burial place of the Prophet Daniel. Near by there is a religious school, the Kulat Paşa Medrese (built in 1570), which houses a small **museum**, with classical and Hittite exhibits, manuscript displays and jewellery.

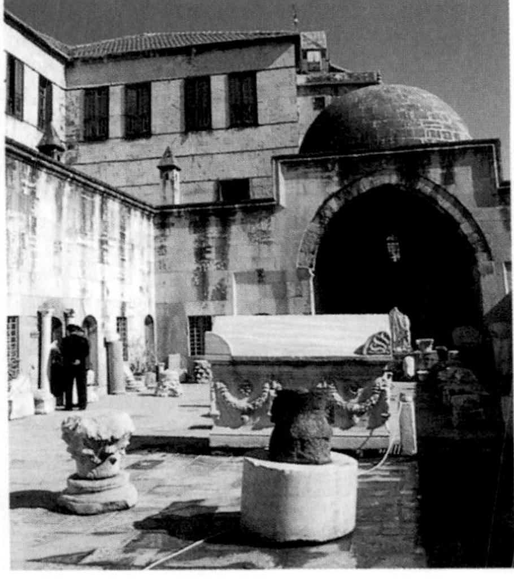

Left: *Artefacts from a past age on display at Tarsus Museum*

The old town surrounds a covered market and open square in which a Roman road is being excavated. Nearby, St. Paul's Well, with supposedly curative water, is theoretically St. Paul's boyhood home.

TOPRAKALE ✪✪

The swirl of modern roads around this formidable fortress emphasizes its strategic importance at the gateway between Syria and Turkey.

Built of forbiddingly dark volcanic rock by Byzantine Emperor Nicophorus II Pocas (963–9), it changed hands numerous times, including a short spell when it was occupied by the crusading Knights of St. John, who redesigned and modelled it on the impregnable Krak des Chevaliers Castle in Syria. It was eventually abandoned in 1337.

29F2
75km (47 miles) east of Adana, at the crossroads of the N-400/E-5 and N-817/E-91
Daily 8:30–5
None
Officially free; guide recommended
Karatepe (➤ 20), Misis (➤ 85), Yılankalesi (➤ 92)

Did you know ?

Born in 356BC, Alexander was the eldest son of Philip II of Macedon. Bent on restoring Greece to former glories, his first action on succeeding to the throne was to gather an army and march east to liberate Asia Minor from the Persian king, Darius the Great. Over the next nine years he amassed a great empire, but died of a fever in Babylon at the age of 32.

UZUNCABURÇ (OLBA/DIOCAESARIA) ✪✪

29E2
30km (19 miles) north of Silifke
Open access
Simple café in the village (£)
Dolmuş from tourist office or Atatürk Square, Silifke
None
Moderate (if caretaker is present)
Silifke (➤ 86)

Now a remote upland village, whose name means 'high tower', after its imposing 22.5m (74ft), five-storey Hellenistic tower (late 3rd century BC), this settlement has been here since Hittite days. In about 295BC, Seleucid ruler, Seleukos Nikator (321–280BC) built a temple to Zeus, the earliest in Asia Minor to use a colonnade; several Corinthian columns still stand. Over the next century its priests gained power as a dynasty of priest-kings, the Teukrides, who established the town of Olba around the temple. They continued to rule under Roman control, although the town changed its name during Vespasian's reign (AD69–79) to Diocaesarea. The ruins, scattered around and to the north of the village, include a Hellenistic pyramid tomb, Roman colonnaded street and monumental arch, a 2nd-century AD theatre, a nymphaeum (fountain) connected to a water supply network still used today, a temple of Tyche and the necropolis.

If you're thirsty, try one of the area's specialities, *kenger kahve* (coffee made from acanthus) or *pekmez* (concentrated grape juice). Local crafts include rugs, leather bags, embroidery and *meşe külü* soap, made from oak ash.

YILAN KALESİ (SNAKE CASTLE) ✪✪

29F2
48km (30 miles) east of Adana, 3km (2 miles) south of the N-400
Officially daily 8.30–5, unofficially open access
Café/restaurant in the car park (£)
Dolmuş to the turn off the N-400
None
Inexpensive
Karatepe (➤ 20), Misis (➤ 85), Topprakale (➤ 91)
Gruelling climb over rocks from car park to walls

This splendid medieval castle, all bastions and battlements, with well-preserved dungeons and living quarters, is one of many built to defend the plains east of Adana in the 13th century, possibly by Leo III (1270–89) while he was crown prince, and the area was a breakaway Armenian state. Its name comes from a local legend that it was the lair of an evil half-man, half-snake, eventually killed in Tarsus while attempting to kidnap the king's daughter.

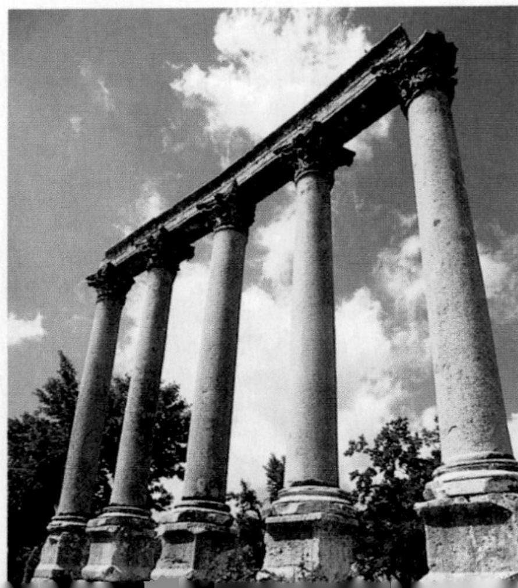

A temple fit for kings—the Corinthian colonnade at the temple of Zeus, Uzuncaburç

Where To...

Above: *A banana stall on the roadside, Anamur*
Right: *The traditional sounds of the Antalya musician*

Lycia

Prices
The price of meals varies more according to location and type of food than choice of restaurants. Tourist areas are invariably more expensive and some are definitely overpriced. Expect to pay considerably more for fresh fish. The cost of alcoholic drinks has risen sharply, and even cheaper table wines are rarely under 30 YTL per bottle. Prices rise regularly. The following price ranges are based on the cost of an average two-course meal (eg *meze*, *kebab*, salad and bread) with non-alcoholic drinks.

£ = 10–20 YTL
££ = 20–40 YTL
£££ = over 40 YTL

One of the greatest delights of a holiday in Turkey is the food, which is excellent, extremely healthy (➤ 50–1), and can be sampled during leisurely afternoons and evenings at a table on an outdoor terrace in a shady garden overlooking the sea.

Demre (Kale)

Güneyhan Restaurant (£)
Simple but pleasant restaurant, with outdoor terrace, well placed beside St. Nicholas's Church.
✉ Gökyazı Mah, Müze Caddesi No 28 ☎ 0242 871 5019 ⌚ All year, lunch and dinner

Simena Restoran (£)
The tables look set for the masses, but they welcome individuals. Standard but reliable fare.
✉ Gökyazı Mah, Müze Caddesi No 23 ☎ 0242 871 3810 ⌚ All year, lunch and dinner

Fethiye

Meğri Lokantası (££)
A long-running favourite with a large terrace and excellent seafood, *meze* and grills.
✉ Likya Sokak 8–9 ☎ 0252 614 4046 ⌚ All year

Marina Lokantası (££)
A well-established and attractive fish restaurant, this occupies one of the best sites in Fethiye, on the promenade, beside the fishing harbour. Perfect for a meal anytime, it serves excellent food to allcomers.
✉ Kordon Boyu ☎ 0252 614 1106 ⌚ All year

Yacht Restaurant (££)
One of Fethiye's few places for banquets and evening entertainment, this venue is popular with groups and there is often traditional dancing and music. Fish is a specialty.
✉ Yat Limanı (yacht harbour, behind the PTT) ☎ 0252 614 7014 ⌚ All year

Yelken Restaurant (££)
Excellent homemade dishes and Turkish cuisine. They prepare and serve fish and seafood particularly well.
✉ Kordon Gezi Yolu (behind Post Office) ☎ 0252 614 5010 ⌚ All year, lunch and dinner

Finike

Amfora Balık Evi (££)
Newest and snazziest restaurant in Finike. Smart interior, white linen table cloths, clean as a whistle and the freshest fish at the most reasonable prices.
✉ Finke Bulvarı (opposite harbour entrance) ☎ 0242 855 3880 ⌚ All year, lunch and dinner

Birlik Restaurant (£)
This is an simply-styled *meyhane* with carefully prepared dishes and is much patronized by locals. Try the *hibeş*, an Antalya regional specialty made of *tahini* (sesame oil and hot pepper paste).
✉ Akın Sok ☎ 0242 855 3184 ⌚ All year, daily, lunch and dinner

Deniz 2 (£)
This restaurant has been going for years, and is a typical, simple local restaurant with cheerful checked tablecloths and better-than-average Turkish food.
✉ Finke Bulvarı (opposite the harbour) ☎ 0242 855 2282 ⌚ All year, daily, lunch and dinner

Kalkan

Aubergine (Patlican) (££)
A pleasant restaurant on the harbour, serving Turkish, Ottoman-style and international dishes.
✉ Harbourfront ☎ 0242 844 3332 ⏲ Summer only, lunch and dinner

Belgin's Kitchen (££)
The best of Turkish cookery, with mouthwatering *börek*, *köfte* and *mantı*, served Ottoman-style reclining on cushions and carpets.
✉ Yaliboyu Mahallesi ☎ 0242 844 3614 ⏲ Summer only, lunch and dinner

Bezirgan Kitchen (£)
The family does all the cooking and bread-baking here. Everything is traditional and tasty and cooked fresh to order. Pretty tables outside in summer.
✉ Yaliboyu Mahallesi ☎ 0242 844 2106 ⏲ All year, lunch and dinner

Korsan Restaurant (££)
Traditional *meze* dishes and roast lamb. Fish is also well presented and delicious. Just keeps getting better.
✉ Yacht Harbour ☎ 0242 844 3622 ⏲ All year, lunch and dinner

Kaş

Blue House (££)
The charming owner cooks everything herself and you are like a guest in her house. Tables are on the tiny terrace with a magical view. Traditional Ottoman dishes.
✉ Sandıklı Sokak No. 9 ☎ 0242 836 2171 ⏲ Jun–Oct only

Eriş (££)
Going for almost 50 years, Yusuf Eris' menu has changed little over the years and he is unfailingly helpful.
✉ Gürsoy Sokak No 13 ☎ 0242 836 1057 ⏲ All year, lunch and dinner

Hanımeli Café (£)
Home cooking as good as it gets. Simple food but typical Turkish specialties.
✉ Arka Sokağı (behind the PTT) ☎ 0242 836 2818 ⏲ All year, lunch and dinner

Mercan (££)
This restaurant adjoins the harbour and serves first-class food, including spit-roasted lamb. Prices are very high but the location and atmosphere compensate.
✉ Hükümet Caddesi Yat Limanı ☎ 0242 836 1209 ⏲ All year, lunch and dinner

Oba Ev Yemekleri (£)
Mum cooks, her sons wait tables and the daughter ladles out huge portions of beef stew and lentil soup in this delightfully informal family restaurant away from the seafront. The traditional Turkish stews make a welcome change from *kebabs* and salad, and there is a shady terrace behind.
✉ Çukurbağli Caddesi ☎ 0242 836 1687 ⏲ All year, lunch and dinner

Sun Café Bar and Restaurant (££)
The Turkish food is consistently, interesting, original and good here. They are known as much for their steady, fair prices as good menu. Cozy and intimate in winter; leafy, terraced garden in summer.
✉ Hükümet Caddesi ☎ 0242 836 1053 ⏲ All year, lunch and dinner

What's What
There are several categories of restaurant, starting with the all-encompassing *restoran*. A *lokanta* is a cafeteria serving a variety of stews kept warm in a bain-marie. A *çorbacı* specializes in soup, a *kebapcı* in döner kebabs (found on many street corners) and a *köfteci* in meatballs. A *meyhanĕ* is a wine bar that serves *mezeler* and simple dishes. The rougher ones are for men only.

Meals
Breakfast (*kahvalti*) is served from 7.30 to 10am and consists of bread, cheese, olives, tomatoes and honey, with tea or coffee. Late risers, the extra hungry or the laidback often enjoy the same—known as 'Second Breakfast.' Civil servants take a lunch (*öğle yemeği,*) break from 12 noon to 1pm, but in general Turks just eat when they're hungry, and cheap and cheerful restaurants are open all day for large or small meals. Snacking is endemic. Dinner (*akşam yemeği*, served from 7 to 10pm) is a sit-down hot meal. For typical courses ➤ 50–1.

Kayaköy

Kaya Wine House (££)
Renovated stone cottage that serves memorable meals and stars as a wine house. Barbecue evenings in summer. This is local cuisine with homely touches in stews and roasts. The house specialty is lamb. Also a beautiful garden.
✉ Gökçeburun Mahallesi No. 70 ☎ 0252 618 0454/612 0476 🕐 All year, lunch and dinner

Kekova

Kekova Restaurant (£)
Hot and cold traditional Turkish fare. The mixed seafood grill is delicious and for hearty eaters.
✉ On the harbour ☎ 0242 874 2022 🕐 All year, lunch and dinner

Kemer

Akdeniz (£)
Built like a scout hut, with a basketball court beside it, this barn of a restaurant on the seafront looks grim in winter but comes into its own in season, when the outdoor terrace is lit and the weather is balmy. The food is standard Turkish grills and seafood.
✉ Deniz Caddesi 7 ☎ 0242 814 1219 🕐 All year, lunch and dinner

Marina (££)
One of the more established restaurants in town, serving the marina on which it stands, but always ready to welcome refugees from all-inclusive catering. The cuisine is Turkish, the food is good and you can join the locals propping up the small bar in the evenings.
✉ Yat Limanı (on the edge of the marina) ☎ 0242 814 1192

Marmaris

Antique Café and Bar (£££)
One of Marmaris' smartest restaurants has luxurious, imaginative cooking to suit international tastes. Seafood, salads and grills are a work of art. Reservations are recommended for tables in summer.
✉ Netsel Marina ☎ 0252-413 2955 🕐 All year round, lunch and dinner

Birtat (£££)
Joins the floral-print and bamboo brigade along the harbour-front promenade, but they have been in business for 40 years and the cooking is top notch.
✉ Barbaros Caddesi ☎ 0252 412 1076

Dede (££)
Thoroughly touristy place at the tourist office end of a long line of seafront restaurants. The huge menu, in English, German and Russian, boils down to the usual Turkish selection of chicken, fish and *kebabs*. Indoor and outdoor tables.
✉ Barbaros Caddesi 15
☎ 0252 413 1289
🕐 8AM–midnight

Taraça (££)
A restored house in the old Greek quarter of Marmaris, Taraça is away from the clutch of harbour restaurants and serves immaculate, imaginative dishes. The 'bistro' touch enlivens the Turkish-style cooking.
✉ 30 Sokak No 11
☎ 0252 411 3999

Ölüdeniz

Beyaz Yunus (White Dolphin) (£££)
Far and away Fethiye's

classiest restaurant in both aesthetic and culinary terms. Magnificent setting above the eastern end of Ölüdeniz beach with Mediterranean garden, many festive specialties and the freshest of fish.
✉ Ölüdeniz ☎ 0252 617 0068 🕐 May–Oct

Restaurant La Turquoise (££)
Poolside restaurant, with live Turkish music. The ambience is fine and the attempt at French cuisine valiant.
✉ Montana Pine Resort ☎ 0252 616 6366 🕐 Lunch and dinner

Şadırvan (££)
Located inland from the main beach area, this restaurant is set in a lovely forest. Outdoor dining in summer, fireplace in winter. Well-cooked meals are better value than those beachside.
✉ Çarşı Meydanı (main square), Hisarönü/Ovacık ☎ 0252 616 6140 🕐 All year, lunch and dinner

Olympos/Ulupınar

Blue and White Hotel and Restaurant (£)
Located near the Chimaera flame, in the village of Çiralı, this is the most sedate place to eat in the area. The passable food is served in a nice atmosphere. Outdoor dining and bar.
✉ Çiralı ☎ 0242 825 700 🕐 Summer only, dinner

Park Restaurant (££)
Wonderful country restaurant in a converted mill, with a shady terrace, trout so fresh it's still swimming, seafood stews and Turkish dishes.
✉ Ulupınar Köyü, Ulupınar (near the turning off the main road, 30km west of Kemer) ☎ 0242-825 7213 🕐 All year lunch and dinner

Ulupınar K Kayalar (£)
A string of restaurants here offer fresh trout. This is the best one and they do the trout any way you want. Very basic, hugely economical and also has *şiş kebap*, flambéed dishes and quail (*bildircin*).
✉ Main Road on left (32km/20 miles west of Kemer), set down the hill, watch carefully for sign ☎ 0242 825 0010 🕐 All year lunch and dinner

Patara

Golden Restaurant (£)
Popular, basic Turkish restaurant right in the middle of the village, attached to one of the best local *pansiyons*. Trout normally features on the menu beside the kebabs.
✉ Gelemiş Köyü ☎ 0242 843 5162 🕐 Summer only, lunch and dinner

Saklıkent

Hüseyin Güseli'in Yeri (£)
Family-run restaurant offering Turkish pancakes and grills, all cooked traditionally over a wood fire.
✉ On the approach road to Saklıkent Gorge ☎ 0252 636 8113 🕐 Summer only, lunch and dinner

Yaka Park (££)
A restored windmill stands at the centre of this park, trout farm and restaurant, with the fish wriggling through fresh-water canals. Popular with tour groups.
✉ Yaka Köyü ☎ 0252 638 2011 🕐 Summer only, lunch and dinner

The Offal Truth
The Turks believe in using every part of the animal. Liver is particularly common, and Arnavut Ciğer, the gourmet version, cooked with onions and herbs is a popular *meze*. Two of the most common dishes which the squeamish might want to avoid are *beyin salatası*, a salad of sliced, marinaded brains, and *işkembe corbaşı*, tripe soup which tastes like warm lard with added flour. Served with raw garlic and vinegar, it supposedly relieves a hangover. Street-sellers offer a rôtisserie of sheep intestines known as *kokoreç*.

Pamphylia, Cilicia and the Hatay

Noah's Feast
After Noah had sailed for 40 days and 40 nights, the flood waters finally began to subside. To celebrate, Mrs Noah put together a grand feast containing all 40 ingredients left on the Ark. The resulting dessert, Aşure, is a thickened pudding made with cracked wheat, pulses, fruit and nuts. It is found in pudding shops (*muhallebi*), although less often on restaurant menus, and is served as a celebratory dish throughout Turkey, associated particularly with the end of the 10-day fast on the 10th day of the Islamic month of Muharram.

Pamphylia

Alanya

Arzum Mantı Evi (£)
Plain, honest, cheap home cooking, specializing in *mantı* (Turkish ravioli). Vegetarian options available.
✉ Atatürk Caddesi ☎ 0242 513 9393

Bistro Bellman (£–££)
Huge harbour-front restaurant, whose Swedish-Turkish owner serves pork, Scandinavian cuisine and well-prepared Turkish dishes.
✉ Harbourfront ☎ 0242 512 1992 🕐 All year, lunch and dinner

Hasan Baba Restaurant (££)
A family affair with real culinary flair. Fish and veal specialties and some international dishes. Kid's menu and free ice-cream for teenies.
✉ Saray Mahallesi, Spor Caddesi 11 ☎ 0242 522 5473 🕐 All year, open am to late

İskele Bar and Restaurant (££)
There is a very good selection of international and local dishes here. This is Alanya's flagship restaurant and is always busy. The view of the old shipyard is superb. They have live music in the evenings.
✉ İskele Caddesi ☎ 0242 513 1822 🕐 All year, lunch and dinner

Odeon (££)
Calm, secluded garden restaurant, tucked away from the street behind an old Ottoman mansion. The Turkish-German owners provide excellent Turkish food with a little continental polish.
✉ Damlataş Caddesi 32 ☎ 0242 513 1354

Yakamoz (£££)
Attractive, busy fish restaurant and café. It is not cheap but excellent food and fine harbour views make it an altogether wonderful dining experience.
✉ İskele Caddesi 39 ☎ 0242 512 2303 🕐 All year, lunch and dinner

Yeni Köşk (££)
Set among banana trees with a panoramic view over Alanya, they whip up wonderful steaks, grills and fish. Turkish nights two nights a week. Playground for kids.
✉ K. Hasbahçe Mahallesi, Yayla Caddesi ☎ 0242 522 5393 🕐 All year, open from 9am until late

Alarahan

Alarahan (£)
Following a millennium of tradition, this restaurant, right beside the ancient caravansarai, offers a full range of meals (including breakfast), a pretty terrace overlooking the river, a souvenir shop and, for the more active, whitewater rafting. It is well outside Alanya and caters primarily for tourist groups and tours.
✉ Alarahan Yanı, Çakallar Köyü ☎ 0242 547 8252 🕐 All year, breakfast, lunch and dinner

Antalya

Antalya Balık Evi (Antalya Fish Place) (£)
You eat only fish here but it is the freshest possible and they will cook it any way you ask. Very popular and always

busy. One of the most reasonably priced places to eat fish, yet still centrally located.

✉ Yeni Halk Pazarı/Dogu Garaj (covered market next to the city bus and dolmuş terminal) ☎ 0242 321 0116

China Garden (£££)

People come from far and wide to eat here. The Chinese food is outstanding and the giant prawns are succulent and fresh. The Peking Duck is highly recommended. One of Antalya's outstanding dining experiences, with literally hundreds of items on the menu.

✉ Konyaaltı Cad. (inside Atatürk Kültür Parkı) ☎ 0242 248 7835 🕒 All year, lunch and dinner

Kırk Merdiven Restaurant (££)

In the centre of the old town, this unassuming restaurant serves fish, international and Turkish dishes lovingly and attentively prepared. Prices are fair and they don't hassle you if you want to read the menu first. In winter, they have a fireplace and, in summer, a leafy terrace.

✉ Selçuk Mah, Musalla Sokak 2 ☎ 0242 242 9686 🕒 All year, lunch and dinner

Konyaaltı Promenade

The beach area, west of Antalya, has been transformed into an urban showpiece, with outdoor cafés, trendy kiosks and tea gardens every few metres. The area is much enhanced by palm trees and shrubs. A 'boardwalk' means that all of Antalya can jog, bicycle, sit or stroll along most of the 7-km (4-mile) stretch of seaside. It is a great place to see a cross section of Turkish life and enjoy yourself as well.

Kral Sofrası (King's Table) (££)

Old-established local favourite, serving excellent Turkish and international food on a terrace overlooking the old harbour. Advance booking recommended.

✉ Old Harbour, Kaleiçi ☎ 0242 241 2198 🕒 Daily, lunch and dinner

La Trattoria (£££)

An Italian trattoria owned by Turkish-Scottish folk. The décor is pleasing, the service friendly and efficent and the food, including sticky puddings, delicious.

✉ Fevzi Çakmak Caddesi 3/C (opposite the Belediye) ☎ 0242 243 3931 🕒 Daily, lunch and dinner

Met Fish Restaurant (££)

Popular with local families and businessmen, this unassuming clifftop fish restaurant offers delicious seafood and sea views in the popular hotel district of Lara.

✉ Lara Yolu, Lara ☎ 0242 321 1828 🕒 Daily, lunch and dinner

Parlak Restaurant (£)

Spit-roasted chicken is the specialty here, but they will willingly cook anything you want—and efficiently. The salads are great and so is Antalya's spicy *meze, hibeş*. Inside is more comfortable than sitting by the flaming spit outside.

✉ Kazım Özalp Sokak No. 7, Zincirli Han ☎ 0242 241 6554 🕒 Daily, lunch and dinner

7 (Yedi) Mehmet (££)

Antalya's landmark eatery began life in the 1940s as a soup kitchen. Perfectly cooked Turkish dishes and flawless service. Grand views from outdoor tables.

✉ Atatürk Kültür Parkı No. 333 ☎ 0242 238 5200 🕒 Daily 10am–midnight

Meze

If you don't speak Turkish, don't worry. It is easy to put together a delicious meal from the huge variety of hot and cold *meze* (starters) that are normally laid out in a chilled cabinet or brought to the table for you to choose. There is ample choice for vegetarians. Simply point to the selection of dishes you want, then add bread and salad.

Simplicity
You can eat very well in Turkey almost everywhere. On the whole, Turks prefer simple, fresh foods without sauces or garnishes. Look for places where the Turks eat, and ignore the décor, which is not always inspirational. Some restaurants do not serve alcohol; those that do charge heavily—taxes on alcohol run at 300–400 per cent. However, there is now a large selection of foreign-owned restaurants in large cities, and cafés, bistros and wine bars are growing in numbers. Many of the large tourist complexes overplay the open buffet option. However, there are also globally recognized hotels which feature outstanding à la carte menus. You can eat to gourmet standards, but expect to pay accordingly.

Aspendos

Aspendos Restaurant (££)
Popular restaurant near the ruins, with a shady terrace overlooking the river. Predictable, dependable Turkish cooking but it can be pricey and the place gets very crowded during the Aspendos Festival.
On the road to the ruins 0242 735 7088 Officially open all year

Belkıs Restaurant (££)
Housed in a simple building down near the river, the food here includes an imaginative selection of Turkish dishes, such as stews presented in attractive earthenware dishes. Wines are good and, with Aspendos Restaurant, they have theatre-going clientèle to themselves.
Belkıs Köyü, on the road to the ruins 0242 735 7263 Summer only, lunch and dinner

Duden Şelâlesi

Arkadaş Alabakık Çiftliği (£)
Charming, simple fish restaurant up a rocky track near the waterfalls. Select your trout from one of the hotel pools, then eat it beside the river. A true rural idyll.
Duden Şelalesi, on the Varsak road north of Antalya Summer only

Köprülü Kanyon

Ada Insel (£)
Stop just before you reach the canyon proper to enjoy a quiet and peaceful lunch on this shady riverside terrace, untroubled by persistent tour guides. The food is simple (fish—probably local trout—kebabs and salad) but good, and the owners friendly and unobtrusive. Rafting can be arranged from here.
Köprülü Kanyon Yolu Üzeri, Beşkonak 0242 765 3389 All year, lunch and dinner

Side

Afrodit Restaurant (££)
A pleasant. lively garden terrace restaurant overlooking the yacht harbour, with a good selection of *meze.*
Old Harbour 0242 753 1171 All year, lunch and dinner

Liman (££)
Wonderfully situated, with an outdoor terrace beside the harbour, this seemingly simple restaurant serving a standard Turkish and international menu has a few tricks up its sleeve to ensure a thoroughly entertaining evening with excellent food. For those with a hearty appetite try the towering fish platter.
71 Liman Caddesi 0242 753 1168 All year, lunch and dinner

Nergiz (££)
On the main square beside the harbour, this is one of the smartest restaurants in town, its two storeys open-air in summer, decorated with carpets and wicker furniture and serving a good version of the normal Turkish menu, with the added bonus of lobsters.
Liman Caddesi, Selimiye Köyü 0242 753 1467 All year, lunch and dinner

Ockbaşi Restaurant
Away from the seafront, near the Turkish baths. A garden and children's playground add to the Ottoman specialties on the menu. Vegetarian and children's menus available.
Zambak Sok 0242 753 1810

Toros Motel Restaurant (££)
Good Turkish food in front of the old harbour.
Liman Caddesi 0242 753 2005

Cilicia and the Hatay

Adana

Üç Kardeşler (£)
Good portions of soups, stews and other Turkish dishes, this is the most central branch of their trio of restaurants.
✉ İnönü Caddesi, Özel I'dare Işhanı, Kat 7, No 702 ☎ 0322 359 2929 🕐 All year, lunch and dinner

Uğur Lokantası (£)
This is your bargain basement for basic home-cooking, stews, kebabs and takeaway.
✉ Sular Yolu, Spor Kulübü Altı (under the Sports Club) ☎ 0322 453 4822 🕐 All year, 24 hours

Yeni Onbaşlar Restoran (££)
This is about the best of the bunch of not-so-exciting eateries in Adana. Typical Turkish fare served in busy and noisy surroundings. No spirits, but serves beer.
✉ Atatürk Bulvarı, Dörtyolağzı ☎ 0322 363 2547 🕐 All year, lunch and dinner

Anamur

Astor Restaurant (£)
Shady outdoor restaurant, with tables under trees, right on the beachfront, serving *meze*, grills and fish.
✉ İskele Mah, İnönü Caddesi, ☎ 0324 814 2280 🕐 Summer only, lunch and dinner

Çelıkler/Kale (£)
A small restaurant across the road from the castle, with a pleasant, shady terrace screened by lemon trees. Simple but well-presented food and a friendly host who will also take you round the castle. There is a small *pansiyon* in summer.
✉ Mamure Kalesi Karşisi, İskele 🕐 All year, lunch and dinner

Antakya

Anadolu (££)
The décor here is unimpressive, but don't be fooled—this unassuming place offers a broad range of *meze* and a wide variety of grills and kebabs.
✉ Hurriyet Caddesi 50/C, ☎ 0326 215 1541 🕐 All year, lunch and dinner

Antakya Ev Restoran (££)
Owned by a local journalist, this is one of Antakaya's most atmospheric eateries and perfect for tucking into the hot, spicy foods of the east. Excellent grills, *meze* and salads served in a restored period house. Private rooms are available for groups.
✉ Silahli Kuvvetli Caddesi ☎ 0326 214 1350 🕐 All year, lunch and dinner

Sultan Sofrasi (££)
Friendly, neighbourhood restaurant on the river, which offers a limited range of *meze*, some excellent soups and casseroles and kebabs.
✉ İstiklal Caddesi 20/A ☎ 0326 213 8759 🕐 All year, lunch and dinner

Mersin

Ali Baba 1 Restaurant (££)
A convenient place to eat after shopping especially as it is located by the main car park entrance.
✉ Uluçarsi Otopark Girisi Karsisi ☎ 0324 233 3088

Tarsus

Şellale (££)
This is the grandest of several restaurants and cafés surrounding the cooling waterfall. The terrace overlooks the falls and the food is excellent, with a wide range of *meze*. Next door is a much simpler café of the same name.
✉ Şellale ☎ 0324 624 8010 🕐 All year, lunch and dinner

Too Much of a Good Thing
The aubergine (or eggplant) is one of the most versatile of ingredients in Turkish cookery. A careless wave at the *meze* counter could land you with five types of aubergine salad. In the 16th century, during the heyday of Ottoman cuisine, the chefs at the court of Süleyman the Magnificent allegedly knew 150 ways of preparing them.

Lycia

Prices

You can save money by contacting a hotel in advance. Agree your price, do all your bargaining and make a firm reservation. You should be able to negotiate a 30–50 per cent reduction out of season. If they seem reluctant to bargain, you can still ask for the corporate, or local (*yerli*) rate. Arriving without advance notice gives you no option but to pay for the *sokak fiyat* (street price), which is the one written on the board at reception. Find out whether prices are per room or per person. Price ranges in this book are per double room with private bathroom.

£ =US$20–50
££ = US$50–100
£££ = over US$100

Pansiyons

The term *pansiyon* covers a huge range of smaller properties, from comfortable 20-room guesthouse charging up to US$50 per room a night to barely furnished rooms sharing a bathroom at the back of a private home for around US$10 a night. In many ways, these offer the best, and certainly most entertaining accommodation for independent travellers, but make sure you know what you are getting before you move in.

Fethiye

Letoönia Hotel and Club (££)

Huge, all-encompassing resort with accommodation in a large hotel block, in villas and in smaller 'club' units with wooden balconies. It also has ten bars, numerous restaurants, two pools, three beaches, all the land and watersports you could desire, a kids' club and a shuttle boat to Fethiye.

✉ PO Box 63, 48300 Fethiye-Muğla; 3km (2 miles) from Fethiye ☎ 0252 614 4966, fax 0252 614 4422; www. letooniaresorts.com 🕲 All year, but restricted facilities in winter

Villa Daffodil (£)

This small, quiet, Ottoman-style *pansiyon* has attractive rooms, a pool, a sauna and a restaurant; 1km (half a mile) from the town centre.

✉ Fevzi Çakmak Caddesi 115 Karagözler ☎ 0242 614 9595, fax: 0242 612 2223 🕲 Summer only

Finike

Presa Di Finica (£££)

375 rooms and 52 private suites, surrounded by citrus groves. Beautiful rooms, sports facilities and state-of-the art convention facilities. Beach directly opposite.

✉ PO Box 31, Sahil Yolu (4km (2.5 miles) from town centre) ☎ 0242 855 5500; fax: 0242 855 5300 🕲 All year

Kalkan

Club Patara/Patara Prince (£££)

This is a luxury class resort with all conveniences and facilities. They have a secluded corner of the bay and feature watersports, tennis courts, a scuba-diving centre and an Italian restaurant.

✉ 2km (1 mile) from the town centre ☎ 0242 844 3920, fax: 0242 844 3930 🕲 All year

Kelebek Hotel (£)

The kind of cozy, well-run hotel you hope to find on holiday. Beautifully furnished and comfortable rooms, plus all the services and about 600m (660yds) from Kalkan centre.

✉ Menteşe Mahallesi No. 4, Karayolları Sokak ☎ 0242 844 3770; fax 0242 844 3731 www.butterflyholidays. co.uk 🕲 All year

Pirat Otel (££)

A medium-sized resort hotel whose two adjacent complexes are very much the centre point in Kalkan. The pool deck and balconies overlook the harbour.

✉ Kalkan Marina ☎ 0242 844 3178, fax: 0242 844 3183 🕲 All year

Kaş

Aqua Princess Hotel (££)

Close to the middle of Kaş, beautifully appointed rooms, pool and restaurant make this a gem of a hotel. Sweeping sea views and the beach is literally a step across the road.

✉ Hükümet Caddesi 71 ☎ 0242 836 2026; fax 0242 836 1044; www. aquaprincess.com 🕲 All year

Ateş Pension (£)

Clean, comfortable, budget-price *pansiyon*. Most rooms are air conditioned; also roof terrace with sea views.

✉ Yeni Camii Caddesi No. 3 ☎ 0242 836 1393/3452 🕲 All year

Habessos Hotel (£££)
Well-appointed hotel within walking distance of all amenities. Own pool and pretty, well-furnished rooms. Quiet neighbourhood. Air conditioning.
✉ Küçükçakıl Mevkii ☎ 0242 836 2024 🕐 All year

Hotel Club Phellos (££)
Vintage hotel but highly recommended. The rooms are spacious and most have balconies and sea views. The pool has a waterslide, the fitness centre is great.
✉ Lycia Caddesi ☎ 0242 836 1953, fax: 0242 836 1890 🕐 All year

Kemer

Most of the hotels in Kemer itself are small and modest; the giants are stretched out along Göynük beach, about 9km (6 miles) east.

Hotel Kaliptus (££)
Friendly and attractive hotel with a pool and two restaurants, within easy reach of town and beach.
✉ Main road into Kemer ☎ 0242 814 2467 🕐 Summer only

Royal Resort Hotel (£££)
One of the smallest and most luxurious of the resorts. This one has 187 rooms, all with balconies, nine villas and four on-site restaurants, as well as pool, sauna, bars and shops.
✉ Göynük ☎ 0242 815 2370, fax: 0242 815 1627 🕐 All year

Sultan Saray (£££)
This vast, complex of nearly 500 rooms is one of a number of 'all-inclusive' resorts. Everything is laid on, from lavish buffets to six bars, tennis and squash courts, pools for adults and children, watersports, films, cabaret, a private beach and a health club.
✉ Göynük ☎ 0242 815 1480, fax: 0242 815 1499 🕐 All year

Ölüdeniz

Club Belcekiz Beach (££)
Colourful, low-rise holiday village on the beach and in walking distance of the lagoon. Facilities include a pool and jacuzzi, shopping mall, bath and pizzeria.
✉ Ölüdeniz 48300, Fethiye-Muğla ☎ 0252-616 6009, fax: 0252-616 6448 🕐 Summer only

Hotel Montana Pine Resort (£££)
Set in the forests in the hills overlooking the lagoon, this timber-frame hotel has 159 rooms and five suites set in gardens. Pools, tennis courts, gym and games room. The beach is 3km (2 miles) away, but there is a shuttle bus.
✉ Ovacık Mah, Ölüdeniz Beldesi, Fethiye ☎ 0252 616 7108, fax: 0252 616 6451 🕐 Summer only

Patara

Beyhan Patara Resort Hotel (£££)
Large, attractive resort, this is Patara's best and most comfortable hotel. Good food and close to the beach and ancient ruins.
✉ Gelemiş Köyü ☎ 0242 843 5096 🕐 All year

Patara View Point Hotel (£)
Charming *pansiyon* just east of town, with a terrace, fine views and shuttle service to the beach.
✉ Gelimiş Köyü ☎ 0242 843 5184, fax: 0242 843 5022 🕐 Summer only

Reading the Stars
Star-ratings were popular in the early days of tourism with the Tourism Ministry and local municipalities both operating their own systems. Confused? Well, so were tourists and hotel owners themselves. Star-ratings are less indicative of a hotel. It is better to be guided by prices, services and facilities. Nowadays, you can usually see what you are getting on the Internet before you arrive at the door, or ask the local tourism information office for suggestions.

What to Expect
There is no shortage of accommodation along the Turkish south coast. Relatively few hotels have real character, but equally, very few are disastrously bad. All the accommodation in this book has showers and toilets en suite, and hot water. However, this may be solar-powered, so check in advance that hot water is 'active' for 24 hours. It is rare to find *pansiyons* on the Mediterranean coast that do not have air conditioning in summer and heat in winter. Don't be shy about asking if they have this and make sure it works when you enter the room. Many hotels are closed from October to April.

Pamphylia, Cilicia and the Hatay

Hotels in Alanya
Many resort hotels for Alanya are clustered along İnçekum beach, about 20km (12 miles) west of the city. New venues are always being added.

Pamphylia

Alanya

Bedesten (££)
Converted 13th-century Seljuk caravansarai on the castle rock, with superb views and pool.
Içkale ☎ 0242 512 1234, fax: 0242 513 7934 All year

Hotel Kleopatra (£)
Thirty six rooms on six floors with an elevator. The beach is just 100m (110yds) away. There is an excellent restaurant that has been recently upgraded to 'gourmet' class. Tropical Bar and swimming pool.
Damlataş Caddesi 17 ☎ 0242 513 3980/81, fax: 0242 513 5494; www.hotelkleopatra.com All year

Kaptan (££)
Located near the Red Tower and overlooking the harbour, this is a 49-room hotel well away from the sandy stretches of holiday clubs. It is an established Alanya landmark and makes a good touring base.
İskele Caddesi 70 ☎ 0242 513 4900, fax: 0242 513 2000 All year

Saray Beach Hotel (£)
Close to all activities and watersports, the 36 rooms here are tastefully furnished and offer good value for money. Restaurants, bars and a swimming pool. Self-catering units are available.
Atatürk Caddesi 163 ☎ 0242 512 6080, fax: 0242 519 0851 All year

Antalya

Alp Paşa Hotel (££)
Atmospheric Ottoman-style building with 60 rooms and a grand honeymoon suite, in the centre of the Old Town. Turkish bath, garden bar. Restaurant serves outstanding à la carte food for lunch and dinner.
Barbaros Mahallesi, Hesapcı Sokak 30 ☎ 0242 247 5676/0045, fax: 0242 248 5074 All year

Dedekonak (£)
Simply restored *konak* (mansion) that offers good, cheap lodging in an old city historic house. There is a courtyard with a fountain.
Kılıçarslan Mah, Hıdırlık Sokak 13 ☎ 0242 247 5170, fax: 0242 247 5170 All year

Güleryüz Hotel (££)
This 32-room hotel near the stadium and the town hall is not luxurious, but it has everything you might want in the way of comfort. Their reputation for friendly, efficient service has been established over many years.
Gençlik Mah, Tinaztepe Caddesi 8, Işıiklar ☎ 0242 248 7923/7984, fax: 0242 241 9424 All year

Hotel Merve (£)
In a backstreet opposite the Yivli Minaret, the Merve is not much to look at but it is economical and convenient. Rooms are simple and so is the breakfast.
Cumhuriyet Caddesi 24 Sokak No 2 ☎ 0242 248 7800, fax: 0242 242 6663 All year

Özmen Pansiyon (£)
Convenient to everything in the heart of Antalya, this 25-room pension is clean and comfortable and family-run. The terrace has wonderful views over the harbour.
Kılıçarslan Mahallesi,

Zeytin Çıkmazı No. 5 ☎ 0242 241 6505, fax: 0242 248 1534; www.ozmenpension.com
All year

Sheraton Voyager (£££)
This large international hotel on the Konyaaltı beachfront is a favourite meeting place for many locals and has good bars and several highly recommended à la carte restaurants. There is an attractive swimming pool and a health centre and gym.
✉ 100 Yil Bulvarı ☎ 0242 243 2432, fax: 0242 243 2462 All year

Manavgat

Club Grand Aqua (££)
Divided into rooms, apartments and studios, Grand Aqua is meticulously managed and tops the comfort quotient. Health and well being are priorities—good facilities for visitors with disabilities—and good food from their own Rani Farm.
✉ Tilkiler Mevkii, Çolaklı ☎ 0242 763 7310; fax 0242 763 8413; www.clubgrandaqua.com
All year

Side

Hanimeli Pansiyon (£)
Tiny, delightful hotel with a marble staircase and garden courtyard. Central.
✉ Turgut Reis Sok ☎ 0242 753 1789 Summer only

Cilicia and the Hatay

Adana

Hotel Seyhan (£££)
One of Adana's top hotels, a glittering tower in the town centre with all trimmings—including conference facilities and a vitamin bar.
✉ Turhan Cemal Beriker Bulv 18 ☎ 0322 457 5810, fax: 0322 454 2834 All year

Inci Hotel (££)
Large, city-centre hotel with well-appointed rooms, friendly, helpful staff, and a bar, nightclub and sauna.
✉ Kurtuluş Caddesi 40
☎ 0322 435 8234, fax: 0322 435 8368 All year

Anamur

Hotel Hermes (££)
Friendly, simply but well-furnished hotel with central heating, air conditioning, a pool and sauna. All rooms have balconies. In season, the disco can be noisy.
✉ İskele Mevkii ☎ 0324 814 3950, fax: 0324 814 3995 All year

Yalı Motel (£)
Attractive, seafront motel right on the beach, with 16 simple *en suite* bungalows, camping and caravan space in shady gardens, and an on-site restaurant and café-bar.
✉ Yalı Mah, İskele ☎ 0324 814 1435, fax: 0324 814 3474
Summer only

Antakya

Antik Beyazıt Hotel (£££)
This gem of a hotel was a Hatay residence and then a courthouse. It was restored in 1998 with 27 rooms on three floors. It is beautifully decorated in period style but with modern services.
✉ Hükümet Caddesi No 4
☎ 0326 216 2900, fax: 0326 214 3089 All year

Büyük Antakya Oteli (£££)
Central, beside the river and in walking distance of the old town, this is Antakya's best hotel: comfortable, smart and friendly.
✉ Atatürk Caddesi 8 ☎ 0326 213 5860, fax: 0326 213 5869
All year

Mersin

Hilton (£££)
Twelve floors with 188 rooms of gleaming American modernity with ocean views.
✉ Adnan Menderes Bulv 3310
☎ 0324 326 5000, fax: 0324 326 5050 All year

Hotels in Antalya
Antalya has numerous small hotels and *pansiyons*, including some refurbished mansions (*konaks*), in the old town. The general brush up and makeover of Antalya's western reaches has brought new and modern hotels to the area. On the east side, the Lara area has the more traditional (and older) holiday clubs but they have many upscale residential apartments and condominiums as their new neighbours.

Carpets and Leather

Bargain Buying

All shops in Turkey expect you to bargain, a leisurely, entertaining activity involving comfortable seats, pleasant conversation and the ubiquitous glasses of tea. Prices start significantly higher in summer, and many places automatically quote in US dollars or Euros. The price often tumbles if you pay cash in any currency. Polite persistence should mean a reduction of around 30–50 per cent.

Leather

Leather goods are somewhat cheaper than you find in Europe or the US. Look carefully and you can find excellent quality at reasonable prices. Top of the range are trendy leather coats and jackets in lambskin (double-face), and beautifully designed handbags and wallets. Leather shoes used to be reasonable and good quality but prices have risen substantially recently. Unfortunately, amongst the quality and reputable Turkish names, fakes and copies of global brands are a coastal phenomenon. They seem authentic enough but price is the give away.

Carpets

Magnificent carpets, from cushion covers to full room size, have been made in Turkey for the last 8,000 years. The best are wool on wool, wool on cotton, silk on cotton or silk on silk. In tufted carpets, the wool should be double-knotted for strength; the more knots per square inch, the better the quality. Flat-weave *kilims* derive from the nomadic traditions, while *sumaks*, *kilims* with a further pattern embroidered on top, usually come from the eastern or Caucasian region. Check the quality and be careful about old carpets—many are aged with the help of tea and sunlight. Good shops will provide a certificate of authenticity and handle shipping.

Alanya

Candan Carpets

A branch of an Istanbul company with a huge stock and knowledgeable staff.

✉ Müftüler Caddesi 9/E
☎ 0242 512 6020

Motif Kilim House

Large quantities of carpet at a range of qualities and prices. Beware of the machine-made offerings.

✉ Hükümet Caddesi, Üçüncü Sokak 8 ☎ 0242 513 0923

Antalya

Antik Bazaar

Established, reliable stockist of a broad range of fine carpets and *kilims*.

✉ Selçuk Mah, İzmirli Ali Efendi Sokak, 12

Bazaar 54

With 11 branches, Bazaar 54 is the world's largest retailer of Turkish carpets, buying direct from and, in some cases, employing the producers. You can pay a deposit, with the balance due only when your carpet arrives safely at your home.

✉ Yat Limani, Kaleiçi 4
☎ 0242 241 0290

Galeri Sumak

One of the most sumptuous of the Old Town carpet shops, with a refreshingly leisurely sales pitch.

✉ Tuzcular Mah Paşa Cami Sokak 18, Kaleiçi ☎ 0242 247 2143

Aspendos

Bazaar 54

Right next to the jewellery centre, Bazaar 54 is a huge, upmarket shopping centre, originally part of Turkey's foremost chain of carpet retailers (see Antalya), but also with large jewellery and leather shops. Carpets are woven on site.

✉ Küçükbelkıs Köyü 07506, Serik ☎ 0242 735 7281
🕒 Daily 9–6

Fethiye

Old Orient Kilim Bazaar

Sumptuous *kilim* shop in a restored Ottoman house.

✉ Karagözler Caddesi 5
☎ 0252 612 1059

Kaş

One of the best shopping centres on the coast, with an excellent range of carpets, jewellery and designer fashion. There is a weekly market on Fridays on the Fethiye Road, just below the bus station.

Atilla Carpets

Located in an old Kaş mansion, there is a good

selection of carpets, *kilims*, saddlebags and unusual Caucasian items.
Liman Caddesi 12 **0242 836 2040**

Magic Orient
Old and new carpets, *kilims* and *sumaks*. Many silk items also available. There is a huge selection here. Prices are fair and reasonable; so they are less open to bargaining.
Hükümet Caddesi 15
0242 836 3150; www.magicorient.com

Perge
Golden Perge Shopping Centre
Huge, tourist-targeted sales emporium with a dazzling selection of carpets and jewellery for those with hefty credit limits.
Aksu, 10 km (6 miles) east of Antalya, near Perge turn-off

Side
Merve Halı Galeri
Well-stocked carpet shop; try out some serious bargaining here.
Köy Meydanı **0242 753 2029**

Nomad Carpet Centre
Main street carpet emporium, one of several competing ferociously for the tourist's custom.
Liman Caddesi **0242 753 1451**

Alanya
Lederland
Massive stock and reasonable prices make this a good hunting ground for leather lovers.
İskele Caddesi 6/B
0242 513 9613

Nihan Leather
Another large outlet, specializing in brightly coloured fashion items.
Keykubat Caddesi 29
0242 513 2031

Antalya
Desa Deri
Turkey's top exporter of leather designer wear, footwear and fashion handbags and accessories. Top-notch leather homewares are the newest line. They produce most of Marks and Spencer's designer leather garments.
Migros Shopping Mall, Arapsu Mahallesi D.2/B9–10
0242 230 1024; www.desa.com.tr

Matraş
Long-established leather manufacturer, producing designer-quality handbags, briefcases and accessories.
Cumhuriyet Caddesi 63
0242 240 3042

Tergan
One of Turkey's top established and upscale producers of men's and women's leather accessories, luggage, handbags and shoes. Committed to quality and high standards.
Atatürk Caddesi 19/B
0242 247 0460; www.tergan.com.tr

Fethiye
Tunç Leather
A comprehensive selection of leather goods.
Paspatur Mevkii, Hamam Sokak **0252 612 3744**

Marmaris
Duygu Bag Shop
Quality leather travel bags, handbags, belts and briefcases in this bazaar shop.
Tepe Mah Rıhtım Sokak 11/A **0252 412 8117**

İlkay Leather Fashion Centre
Very nice selection of good quality ladies' and men's leather fashions, including jackets, trousers and suits.
Gözpınar Sokak 36
0252 412 9466, fax: 0252 413 1290

Tax Refunds
There are over 2,200 tax free shopping outlets in Turkey. You must spend a minimum of 118 YTL in one shop in one day. Ask the retailer for a Global Refund Cheque. When exiting Turkey, have your tax-free invoices and purchases (they must accompany you) ready to show to passport and customs offcials and have your invoice(s) or cheques stamped.
Main airports, seaports and border crossing points have refund offices, who will give you an immediate cash refund. Some of these, however, are banks who work office hours. You can mail your stamped and validated cheque to Global Refund to receive your credit. Refunds do not apply if you exit Turkey more than three months following the month of purchase. Local VAT is 18 per cent but the refund deducts handling expenses and commissions. Refunds average 12 per cent of the purchase price.

Jewellery, Fashion, Books and Gifts

Jewellery
Hidden amongst a sea of mass-market tat are some true delights, with delicate hand-worked chains, exquisite traditional filigree, and even a few genuine antiques. Gold jewellery shops once proliferated but silver sellers now offer original, exquisite and sometimes outrageous designs. The craft is Turkish, but almost all the stones are imported. A few key centres produce magnificent, custom-designed pieces literally fit for kings. Prices are reasonable, but if you are serious about buying, do some homework before leaving home. Otherwise, window-shopping is fun.

Jewellery

Alanya

Akman Jewellery
Gold, silver, precious and semi-precious stones are all on sale in this solid jewellers. Good quality, but few surprises.
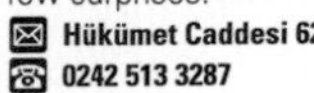
Hükümet Caddesi 62
0242 513 3287

Gold Paradise
In this case, all that glitters is gold—all finely worked and lovely to hold.
Bostancıpınarı Caddesi 12
0242 513 9839

Tiffany
One of the largest and best-known shops in a strip of pricey jewellers. No relation to the New York version.
Hükümet Caddesi 44
0242 512 1069

Antalya

Dösem
Ministry of Culture souvenir shop, with an excellent collection of fine handicrafts from across Turkey, including reproduction ancient jewellery. Other branches at the Antalya Archaeological Museum and Aspendos.
Yacht Harbour, 24 **0242 241 4667**

Aspendos

Aspendos Jewellery Centre
This vast jewellery empire on the approach road to Aspendos is a dazzling sea of magnificent gold, silver and precious stones. The experience begins with a tour of the ground floor workshops, with 180 jewellers working on site (the stones are behind glass), followed by tea and courteous persuasion amidst acres of gleaming cases. Options range from simple charms and silver cartouches with your name in Hittite, to solitaire rocks and custom-designed grandeur. Worth a look anyway.
Küçükbelkıs Köyü 07506, Serik **0242 735 7250**

Fethiye

Erol's Gold
This is a large jewellery emporium with precious and semi-precious stones and the whole range of rings, necklaces, bracelets and wonderful earrings.
Hamam Sokak 7 **0252 614 9251/612 2929**

Telmessos Gold Galerie
They have a lovely selection of gold and precious stones here. European and local designs available.
Atatürk Caddesi 2 **0252 612 2809/2810**

Kaş

Silver Art
Beautiful rings, necklaces and bracelets, as well as objets d'art, are on offer here. There is a good selection of semi-precious stones and many amber items.
İbrahim Serin Caddesi 3/A
0242 836 1186

Topika
Stunning designs in silver and precious stones, with a custom-design service.
Bahce Sokak 4D
0242 836 2363

Marmaris

Vogue Jewellery and Diamond Centre
This is an upmarket emporium of stunning jewels

and precious stones. It is a few kilometres from the town centre, but they have a free shuttle service.

Kemal Elgin Bulvarı

0252 413 4875

Side

Flash Jewellery

Tiny backstreet jeweller with imaginative gold and precious stones worked into pieces.

Liman Caddesi 0242 753 2519

Jasmin Jewellery

Wide-ranging stock and helpful staff, eager to make use of your credit card.

Liman Caddesi 56 0242 753 2258

Fashion, Books and Gifts

Antalya

Ardıc Kitabevi

Foreign language books, magazines and newspapers.

Selekler Çarşısı, 67
0242 247 0356

Fethiye

Fethiye's excellent market attracts people from all the surrounding districts. Tuesday is its busiest and most popular day, as villagers convene with all their produce. It mainly sells food but there are some souvenirs.

between Çarşı Caddesi and Tütün Sokak

Imagine

Excellent bookshop, with a large supply of English-language novels and guides, plus music.

Cumhuriyet Caddesi 9
0252 614 8465

Kalkan

Nazar Seramik

High quality ceramics and porcelain bowls, plates and decorative ware in the hand-painted Kütahya tradition.

Yalıboyu Mahallesi
0242 844 3530

Kaş

Merdiven Kitap Evi

Excellent range of English and foreign language novels and pulp fiction in hardback and paperback. Local guide books and books by local authors.You can also buy secondhand books and stationery.

Merkez Mahallesi, İlk Okul Sokak 4/B 0242 836 3022

Papilio Butik

Owner-designer Sumru goes way back to the region's roots, specializing in gorgeous, free-flowing Grecian-style dresses, many made of local cool cotton fabrics.

Uzun Çarşı Sokak 16/B
0242 836 2895

Tufan Designer

The local tailor turns out lovely tunics, dresses and harem pants for women in cotton and silk. Gondolier-type boating shirts for men are a top-selling item.

İbrahim Serin Sokak
0242 836 2917

Marmaris

Continental

Dedicated solely to Turkish ceramics, mostly plates and vases: some of the hand-painted work is quite beautiful. Packaging is provided. Conveniently located in the bazaar.

Eski Çarşı Sokak 28/A
0252 413 4008

Nur-Bal

Bring home a jar or two of Marmaris honey. This little shop, in a block behind the post office, has a good selection. The dark-coloured, pine (*çam*) honey is the best but flower (*çiçek*) honey is also lovely. Also ask to see some *portakal* (orange) honey, less pure and a light-coloured, sweeter variation.

Fevzi Paça Caddesi 9/C

Shopping in Antalya

Much of the old town is now wall-to-wall carpet, jewellery and ceramic shops, all too often accompanied by very aggressive sales pitches. The fashionable and pricier clothing and specialty shops are along Konyaaltı Caddesi (leading to the Archaeological Museum) and Işıklar Caddesi (by the Stadium). Antalya's tramway system runs conveniently past both areas. Shopping patterns have altered in Antalya since the opening of the large Migros Mall, at the western end of town (past the Sheraton Voyager). All the upmarket shops and market glitter are here and everything is open seven days a week, often until late. More downbeat is the covered People's Market (Halk Pazarı), adjoining the city's local bus terminal, Doğu Garajı.

Children's Activities

What to Eat
Formula and powdered baby food are easily available, but the bottled variety is more difficult to find, and it may be worth bringing a stock of your own. Bottled and carton milk is safe, as is fruit juice, although tap water is not. Impress on your children that even teeth should be cleaned with bottled water. For older children, the Turkish diet is simple and very healthy and there should be few problems. Many restaurants now feature vegetarian dishes and, if not, will usually create something without meat.

Caves

Alanya

Dalmataş Mağarası
The 'Weeping Cave' (➤ 59) is a magical place to take children, with its eerie stalactites and stalagmites.
✉ South end of western beach ⏲ Daily 10–8

Kaş

Blue Cave (Mavi Mağrası)
Located just east of Kaputaş Beach, this is one of the largest sea caves in Turkey. Accessible only by boat. Trips go from Kalkan and Kaş in the summer months.

Theme Parks

Antalya

Aquapark
Belonging to the Dedeman Group, with their hotel next door, Aquapark is free for hotel guests. Impressive range of clover-leaf slides for daredevils, and paddling pools for the timid. Adjoins a leisure centre with bowling alleys, billiards and games machines.
✉ Hotel Dedeman, Lara Yolu
☎ 0242 321 7938
Expensive

Lunapark Funfair
Traditional funfair, with merry-go-rounds, rides and plastic prizes. A severe let-down for children raised on Western theme parks, but a good way of filling an evening.
✉ Konyaaltı
☎ 0242 247 6889
Expensive

Minicity Antalya
Miniature models of Turkey's important mosques, palaces, ancient sites and distinctive landmarks, carefully reproduced at a scale of 1:25. New micro creations are added regularly. A grand day out for all ages.
✉ Arapsu Mahallesi 600 Sokak, Konyaalti ☎ 0242 228 9228 ⏲ Daily 9am–11pm (9–7 in winter) Moderate

İçmeler

Aqualife Water Park
An independent waterpark with no connections to hotels, they have an adventure river, slides, bumper boats and trampolines as well as beach volleyball and other get-wet activities. There is a snack bar.
✉ opposite the PTT in İçmeler
☎ 0252-455 5049
Expensive

Kemer

Aquaworld
Definitely the country cousin of the Antalya park (see opposite), this seafront operation has several small slides and pools.
✉ İskele Caddesi (seafront)
⏲ Daily 9:30–6:30
Expensive

Naturland Eco Park and Resort Hotels
There are two areas here: a 133-room aqua resort which has sports (and courts), a watersports centre, and an aquarium park. Then there is a 56-room country resort with more pastoral pursuits such as an organic farm, petting zoo and ranch club. It is all very rural, green and eco-orientated.
✉ Çamyuva, 8km (5 miles) south of Kemer, off the N-400
☎ 0242 824 6214
⏲ Daily 9–6
Expensive

Evening Entertainment

Much of the evening entertainment along southern Turkey's coastal strip is laid on purely for tourists, and while the place is humming in summer, it is like a ghost town out of season.

Alanya

Auditorium Open Air Disco

Loud, brash but buzzing open-air disco.

✉ Dimçayi Mevkii

Janus Restaurant and Café-Bar

Bright (pink), noisy and cheerful all day, churning out food and drink, from kebabs to burgers and pizzas, with late-night dancing.

✉ Rıhtım Girişi (near the harbour) ☎ 0242 513 2694

Antalya

Birdland Jazz Club

Cool and trendy jazz club in a restored *konak* (mansion), with a breezy terrace overlooking the sea.

✉ Hıdırlık Kulesi Arkası, Hesapçı Sokak, 78 Kaleiçi ☎ 0242 242 01507

Çizgi Café and Bar

The yachting world meets Turkish kitsch in this Old Town bar, where you can lounge on cushions near low tables like an Ottoman potentate, surrounded by nautical memorabilia. Serves good cocktails and some snacks.

✉ Uzun Çarşı 28, Kaleiçi ☎ 0242 248 1549

PM Bar and Underground

Head here if you are young, have too much energy and like deafening noise. The blaring music is rock and Turkish pop, the place is jammed and the alcohol flows freely.

✉ Cumhuriyet Caddesi 59, Sokak 8 ☎ 0242 247 3256

Fethiye

Club Music Factory

Pub, club, bar and disco all rolled into one, the in trends in music and vocal are found in this lovely stone house curtained with ivy.

✉ Hamam Sokak 29, Paspatur ☎ 0252 612 6008

Disco Marina

Popular disco with mirror balls on the ceiling and belly-dancing amongst the entertainments. Air conditioned.

✉ Birinci Karagözler, Yat Limanı Karsısı ☎ 0252 614 9860

Otantik Bar

More mirror balls and plenty of noise to shake the structure of this restored Ottoman house.

✉ Paspatur Mevkii Hamam Sokak ☎ 0252 614 6954

Kaş

Fullmoon Hotel and Disco

An open-air disco, a short way out of town, they have a shuttle float that takes you there and back. Romantic setting overlooking the water and the Peninsula opposite.

✉ Fullmoon Hotel, 1km (half a mile) out of town on Fethiye road ☎ 0242 836 3241

Hi Jazz Bar

New York taxi-driver-turned-bar-owner runs this cozy place. There is outdoor seating in the summer and it is lively with trendy music.

Dancing

All the holiday clubs have discos or disco-bars, some open-air. Most are loud, with a mixed crowd of locals and tourists and, apart from drinks, entrance is usually included in the cost of your package. Many big hotels have their own entertainment, with singing, musicians or authentic Turkish nights. Antalya has a few more stylish cocktail bars with live jazz or piano music. Purchasing alcoholic drinks is becoming increasingly expensive, particularly in bars and restaurants. Most places stay open until 2 or 3am and many close for the winter season.

Film
There are cinemas in all the major towns, and most show the popular recently released blockbusters as soon as they are shown anywhere else in world. Most of these are dubbed into Turkish, but at the major resorts you'll find Hollywood films in English and other European languages. Many of Antalya's high-rise apartments incorporate a public cinema on the ground floor. Each year, during the first week of October, Antalya hosts the Golden Orange Film Festival. Latterly this has included only Turkish films.

Zumrut Sokak 0242 836 3575 Closed in winter

Reggae Bar
Bamboo lounge and exotic cocktails overlooking the picturesque harbour of Kaş. Retired journalist DJ's this popular place with the right mixture of music and romance.
Hükümet Caddesi 10
0242 836 2832

Sun Café Bar and Restaurant
People come here as much to drink and prop up the bar as to eat. This is a popular place with locals who often end their day here on the terrace overlooking the harbour.
Hükümet Caddesi
0242 836 1053

Kemer

Ayışığı Disco
A thumpingly loud and always crowded disco serving everything from rock to jazz.
Moonlight Park, near the marina 0242 814 3250

Marmaris and İçmeler

Bar Street in Marmaris (also known, although rarely, as Hacı Mustafa Sokak) keeps all the decibels in one place. It is loud, fast-moving and easy to move from one bar to the other. This is the most convenient and best bar-crawling and night-clubbing venue on the coast, apart from in-house hotel entertainment.

Beach Club
An indoor disco with DJs providing the music and occasional appearances by professional singers. Very popular and currently the 'in' place.
Uzunyalı Marmaris

Crazy Daisy Bar
Decibels, drinks and dancing, exotic cocktails and psychedelic laser lighting make this a terrific evening venue. There is a more upmarket branch with a cabaret and nightclub at Uzunyalı, on the outskirts of the city.
Bar Street 0252 412 4856

Greenhouse Disco Bar
Great atmosphere, lively (canned) music and wonderful laser show. Snack bar on the premises.
Bar Street 0252 412 0834

Joy
This is a well-established disco in İçmeler and its circular shape makes it easy to identify, situated on the right side of the main road as you come into İçmeler from Marmaris.
İçmeler 0252 455 3302 ***Dolmuş* to Marmaris**

Side

Blues Bar
Warm, friendly bar with an outdoor terrace serving 100 different cocktails.
Cami Sokak 0242 753 1197

Zeppelin Bar
Loud music, large crowds, a hot, sweaty atmosphere and sea views. Of course it is great if you like that sort of thing.
Barbaros Caddesi, 68
0242 753 4323

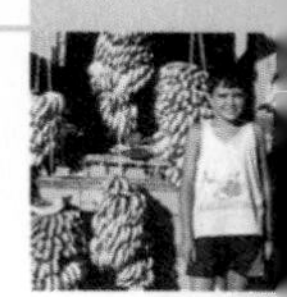

Tours and Activities

Sightseeing Tours

One of the easiest ways to get out and about on the Turkish south coast is to take one of the many half-day, day or short-break tours on offer. Numerous options cover activities from *gület* trips to beach barbecues, intensive history to cultural extravaganzas, visiting nomad encampments to jeep safaris. Walk along the quay and hop on to any one of a dozen boats, or visit one of the many travel agents in the resorts. Do a little homework first to stop yourself being pressurized into a hasty decision and high price by the over-eager salesmen. Few tours operate in winter, but someone will always take you if you have the cash. Just ask around.

Adana

Adalı Turizm

Full travel agency service.

✉ **Stadyum Caddesi 37/C**
☏ **0322 453 7440**

Alanya

Tantur

One of Turkey's big tour operators, they arrange everything for yacht charter, destination tourism, and special-interest holidays.

✉ **Güller Pınarı Mah, 12 Eylül Caddesi, Akdeniz Apartman**
☏ **0242 512 0982/513 3362; www.tantur.com.tr**

Antalya

Akay Travel Service

Tours to hard-to-reach archaeological sights.

✉ **Cumhuriyet Caddesi 54, Solmaz İşhanı, Kat 1** ☏ **0242-243 1700**

Great Jolly Tour

A comprehensive range of touring, yacht and sightseeing services, package tours and tailor-made holidays. A good name and a friendly, efficient attitude.

✉ **Anafartarlar (Gülluk) Caddesi, Saraçoğlu İşhanı**
☏ **0242 247 4660**

Mozaik Tours

Long-established business handling excursions and incoming and outgoing tours. Antalya agents for KTHY, Turkish Northern Cyprus Airlines.

✉ **Cumhuriyet Meydanı, 22 Sokak 8/B** ☏ **0242 243 5555**

Pamfilya

One of the biggest agencies on the coast, they arrange all tours, incoming and outgoing transfers and special-interest package tours and destination travel events.

✉ **30 Ağustos Caddesi 57/B**
☏ **0242-243 1500; www.pamfilya.co.**

Skorpion Turizm

Sightseeing, mountaineering, jeep safaris, trekking, and village tours.

✉ **Fevzi Çakmak Caddesi 12/5**
☏ **0242 243 0890/91**

Stop Tours

Mountain biking, horse-riding, yacht tours and historic sights.

✉ **Dr Burhanettin Onat Caddesi, Yılmaz Sitesi, A Blok, 14** ☏ **0242 322 6557**

Fethiye

Be There Yachting and Travel Agency

Daily excursions, flight reservations and specialist on yachting and *gület* cruises.

✉ **Fevzi Çakmak Caddesi 11/1, Marina** ☏ **0252 614 7711, fax: 0252 614 9119**

Emergencies

There is no need to worry as long as you take sensible precautions. Turkey is basically hygienic and civilized, with good standards of medical care. Children should keep on their hats (against the sun) and shoes (against nasty insects and bits of broken glass), use sunblock, drink plenty of liquids, wash their hands regularly and watch where they put them when scrambling around on the rocks (look out for scorpions or snakes). Take plenty of pills to counteract the inevitable travel sickness on the twisting roads. Ideally, avoid July and August, when the heat is often unbearable and the crowds are at their rowdiest.

Sporting Tours
Most large beach hotels run their own programmes of watersports and either have or provide access to tennis courts, but inland adventure sports such as riding, trekking and whitewater rafting are also growing in popularity. In winter, there is skiing in the Taurus Mountains, a short way inland. Turkey's premier golf course is at Belek, near Aspendos, with access from all the large local hotels, many of which also have their own courses. Some of the general travel agents and tour operators listed above also offer a variety of sporting activities.

Cadianda Tours
They specialize in one- and two-day jeep safaris but also arrange canoeing, fishing trips and private tours.
✉ Babataşı Mah, M Kemal Bulvarı ☎ 0252 614 4150, fax: 0252 612 8655

Kalkan

Adda Tour and Travel Agency
Provides sightseeing, cruises, diving, villa and car rentals.
✉ Yalı Boyu Mahallesi
☎ 0242 844 3610

Armes Turizm
This was Kalkan's first tourism agency and they are still helpful and expert in all aspects of travel and tourism.
✉ Yalı Boyu Mahallesi
☎ 0242 844 3169, fax: 0242 844 3468

Kaş

Bougainville Travel
Cultural tours, trekking on the Lycian Way Walk, boat tours, abseiling in Saklıkent Gorge, and nomadic village safaris. They have their own diving boat and are conscientious about safety and have a good reliability record.
✉ İbrahim Serin Caddesi
☎ 0242-836 3737;
www.bougainville-turkey.com

Dolce Vita Tourism, Travel and Yacht Agency
Adventure tours, trekking, sightseeing and daily trips. Sea-kayaking a specialty.
✉ Cumhuriyet Meydanı 7
☎ 0242 836 1610

Latebreaks Travel Agency
Daily tours, reservations, 'Blue Voyage' cruises, and car rental. Agents for Turkish Airlines. Also handle ticketing for domestic low-cost carriers (► 121)
✉ Hükümet Cadessi 16
☎ 0242 836 1725

Sky Sports
Paragliding specialists.
✉ Liman Sokak ☎ 0242 836 3291

Kemer

Akay
Excursions to local archaeological sites.
✉ Liman Caddesi ☎ 0242 814 4890

Pamfilya Tour
Local branch of the nationwide operator.
✉ Hastane Caddesi 122, Sokak 21/B ☎ 0242 814 1981

Mersin

Bumer Tourism and Travel Agency
Sightseeing excursions, car rental, transfers and ticketing.
✉ Palmiye Mah İsmet İnönü Bulv, Merkon Sitesi N Blok 5
☎ 0324 326 6271

Side

Şelale Tour
Local day trips and regional excursions.
✉ Liman Caddesi ☎ 0242 753 1066

Sporting Tours

Alanya

Alraft Rafting and Riding Club
Whitewater rafting on the Dimçay River and riding expeditions in nearby forests.
✉ Bıçakçı Köyü Mevkii
☎ 0242 513 9155
✉ Azak Hotel
☎ 0242 512 3966

Active Divers
Diving tours, underwater photography and PADI courses, from the Pasha Bay Hotel.
✉ İskele Caddesi 80
☎ 0242 512 8811

Martin Türkay
Mountain- and motorbikes to rent.
✉ Atatürk Caddesi 95/C
☎ 0242-513 5666

Antalya

Get Wet Turizm Limited
Get Wet offers white-water rafting and snow rafting. Also abseiling, trekking, mountain biking, camping and Jeep safaris.
✉ Eski Lar Yolu 198/1 ☎ 0242 324 0855/56; www.getwet.com.tr

Middle Earth Travel
Handles all details for the Lycian Way Walk and the St. Paul Trail, long distance treks.
✉ Gaferli Mahallesi, Cevizler Sokak 20 ☎ 0242 271 2559; www.middleearthtravel.com; www.lycianwaywalk.com; www.stpaultrail.com

Fethiye and Ölüdeniz

There are numerous opportunities here for all sorts of sport, from water-sports on the Ölüdeniz lagoon to paragliding off 1,975m (6,468ft) Mount Babadagi, rafting on the Dalaman and Esen rivers and walking, riding and jeep safaris in the mountains.

European Diving Center
British-run company offering courses and daily dives; PADI.
✉ Atatürk Caddesi ☎ 0252 614 9771

Explora
Jeep safaris, watersports, parascending, scuba-diving, horse-riding and excursions to Rhodes.
✉ Hisarönü, Fethiye
☎ 0252 616 6890
✉ Han Camp, Ölüdeniz
☎ 0252 616 6316

RTT Travel Service
Handles travel, rentals, day trips and excursions.
✉ Marina, Fevzi Çakmak Cadessi 23, Fethiye ☎ 0252 612 0476/614 5700; www.rtt-travelservice.com

Turkish Baths

The *hamam* or Turkish bath is a tradition handed down across the millennia from ancient Rome. It started simply as a way of keeping clean, but then became one of the major social centres of any town, and it remains a place of pampered luxury. Most are open 6am–11pm. Bathing is usually strictly segregated by sex, although a few places offer limited hours for mixed bathing. Many upscale hotels have their own *hamam*.

Alanya

Beyler Hamam
Single-sex and mixed baths and a full massage available.
✉ Bostancıpınarı Caddesi 6
☎ 0242 513 5937

Mimoza Turkish Bath
Get scrubbed clean, hang around in the steam room, and have a massage.
✉ Sugözü Caddesi 19
☎ 0242 513 9193

Antalya

Antalya Yeni Hamamı
Spotlessly clean Turkish baths, with English- and German-speaking staff.
✉ Sinan Mah 1255, Sokak No 3/A ☎ 0242 242 5225

Demirhan Turkish Bath
Clean and modern, with professional massage.
✉ Güllük Caddesi ☎ 0242 243 6196/247 5859

Fethiye

Old Turkish Bath
Single-sex and mixed facilities at this old *hamam* in the bazaar area. Choose between an oil massage and a soap massage.
✉ Hamam Sokak 2, Paspatur Bazaar ☎ 0252 614 9318

Marmaris

Armutalan
Supposedly the largest *hamam* in Marmaris, with jacuzzi, pool and coiffeur.
✉ Cami Avlu quarter, by Karaca Sitesi Armullan
☎ 0252 412 0710

Bath Etiquette
When using the Turkish Baths, undress in the *camekân* (reception area). Full nudity is not usual; wear your swimming costume or request a *peştamal* (sarong). You will also be given a towel and *takunya* (wooden clogs). The main chamber (*hararet*) is a hot steam room, with a large marble slab on which you lie during a face-, foot- and/or full body massage, or a scrub-down with a camel-hair glove. There are private side rooms for washing down first.

What's On When

Oil Wrestling
Yağlı güreş (oil wrestling) is one of Turkey's most bizarre local activities—and the country's national sport. Competitors smear themselves with oil before getting to grips with each other. Local bouts are held throughout the spring and summer, announced by a loudspeaker system, posters and a traditional drummer and *zurna* (oboe-like horn) player. Venues are often open fields just outside town. A collection is taken to raise money for charitable projects.

January/February
Camel-wrestling matches sometimes held in the Demre area (although more common in Aegean region).

May
Silifke Music and Folkore Festival.

May/June
Marmaris Yachting Festival.

June
Alanya International Beach Volley Championships.

June/July
Aspendos International Opera and Ballet Festival (extends into July): huge crowds attend a programme of performances in the magnificent ancient theatre, with big name performers.

July
International Folk Festival, in Antalya and Aspendos.
Manavgat Tourism Festival.

Summer
Oil wrestling (see panel).

September
Kemer Carnival.
Mersin Art and Culture Festival.
Marmaris Tango Festival (second week).
Adana Altın Koza (Golden Boll, as in cotton) Festival.

September/October
Antalya International Akdeniz Song Contest
Kaş–Lycian Culture Festival

October
Altın Portakal (Golden Orange) Film Festival, Antalya.
Alanya International Triathlon Competition: swimming, cycling and running.
International Bodrum Cup Regatta: third week; this is strictly for wooden yachts only.

October/November
Marmaris International Yacht Race Week: last week October to first week in November.

December
Antalya International St. Nicholas Symposium and Festival: this is a very popular programme with lectures, debates and pilgrimage to Demre and Patara.

Moveable Festivals
Turkey celebrates several moveable Muslim festivals and observances. Ramazan (also known as Ramadan) is the month-long fast which is a basic duty of all true Muslims. Between the hours of sunrise and sunset people must abstain from sexual relations, and no food, water nor tobacco must pass the lips (except for the pregnant or infirm). Otherwise, life theoretically goes on as usual. Tourist restaurants remain open, but it is best to be discreet about eating in public. Dusk sees the start of a huge meal. At the end of Ramazan, Şeker Bayramı (the Candy Festival) is a three-day celebration, marked with street parties and the giving and consumption of huge numbers of sweets and pastries. Kurban Bayramı, the more sombre four-day Feast of the Sacrifice, celebrates Abraham's willingness to sacrifice his son Isaac to God. Traditionally, meat is distributed among the poor.

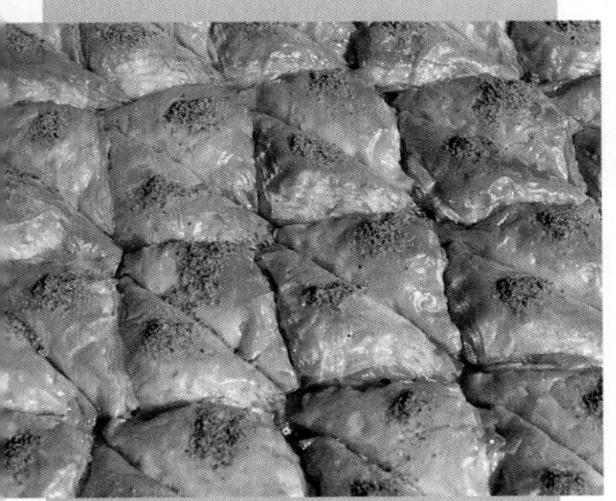

Practical Matters

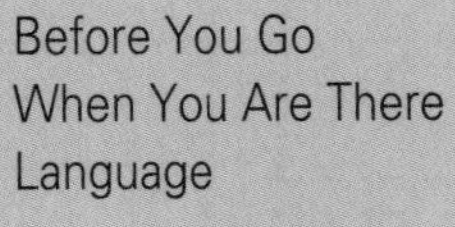

Above: *Baklava—a delicious oriental sweet*
Right: *Old habits die hard in the countryside*

TIME DIFFERENCES

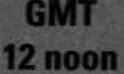

GMT	Turkey	Germany	USA (NY)	Netherlands	Spain
12 noon	2pm	1pm	7am	1pm	1pm

BEFORE YOU GO

WHAT YOU NEED

● Required
○ Suggested
▲ Not required

All visitors require a passport to remain valid for at least six months beyond the date of entry unless you have Turkish nationality, when a Turkish ID card is sufficient.

	UK	Germany	USA	Netherlands	Spain
Passport/National Identity Card	●	●	●	●	●
Visa (obtainable upon arrival—check regulations before your journey)	●	▲	●	●	●
Onward or Return Ticket	○	○	○	○	○
Health Inoculations (tetanus and polio)	▲	▲	▲	▲	▲
Health Documentation	▲	▲	▲	▲	▲
Travel Insurance	○	○	○	○	○
Driving Licence (EU or International)	●	●	●	●	●
Car Insurance Certificate (if own car)	●	●	●	●	●
Car registration document (if own car)	●	●	●	●	●

WHEN TO GO

Antalya

High season

Low season

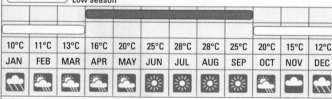

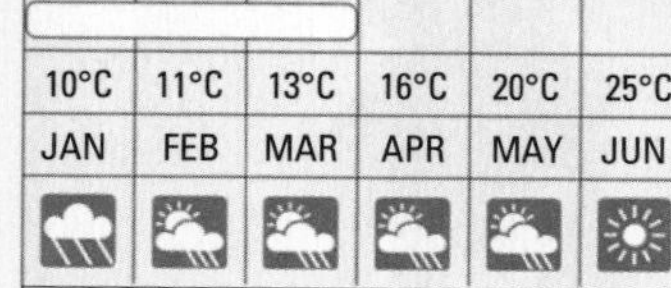

JAN	FEB	MAR	APR	MAY	JUN	JUL	AUG	SEP	OCT	NOV	DEC
Low season	Low season	Low season	High season	High season	High season	High season	High season	High season	Low season	Low season	Low season
10°C	11°C	13°C	16°C	20°C	25°C	28°C	28°C	25°C	20°C	15°C	12°C
Wet	Sun/Showers	Sun/Showers	Sun/Showers	Sun/Showers	Sun	Sun	Sun	Sun	Sun/Showers	Cloud	Wet

Very wet   Wet   Cloud   Sun   Sun/ Showers

TOURIST OFFICES

In the UK
Turkish Information Office
1st Floor,
Egyptian House,
170-73 Piccadilly,
London, W1V 9DD
☎ 020 7355 4207;
www.tourismturkey.org

In the USA
821 United Nations Plaza,
New York, NY 10017
☎ 212/687-2194/5

Website
www.turizm.gov.tr

1717 Massachusetts Ave NW,
Suite 306,
Washington, DC 20036
☎ 202-429 9844/9409

EMERGENCY (Inc. Ambulance) 112

FIRE 110

POLICE (*Polis*)—in town 155

(*Jandarma*)—in country 156 TRAFFIC POLICE 154

WHEN YOU ARE THERE

ARRIVING

Turkish Airlines has connecting scheduled services via Istanbul to all domestic airports in Turkey. Onur Air, Atlas Air and Fly Air also have low cost scheduled services between major hubs. In high season, there are charter flights from across Europe.

Antalya Airport
Kilometres to city centre

15 kilometres (9 miles)

Journey times

Train	N/A
Bus	15 minutes
Car	15 minutes

Dalaman Airport
Kilometres to Fethiye

50 kilometres (31 miles)

Journey times

Train	N/A
Bus	N/A
Car	Car to Fethiye 1½hr

MONEY

Turkey changed its currency in 2004, knocking off many noughts. The currency is the Yeni Turk Lira (YTL; new Turkish Lira) which was, at the time of writing, roughly equivalent in value to the euro. Coins (*kuruş*) are in 1, 5, 10, 20, and 1 YTL denominations. Notes are in 1, 5, 10, 20, 50 and 100 YTL units. ATMs are everywhere and credit cards widely accepted. Travellers' cheques attract a discretionary commission if cashed at banks. Nobody refuses cash and most tourist shops will quote in lira, euros, US dollars or pounds.

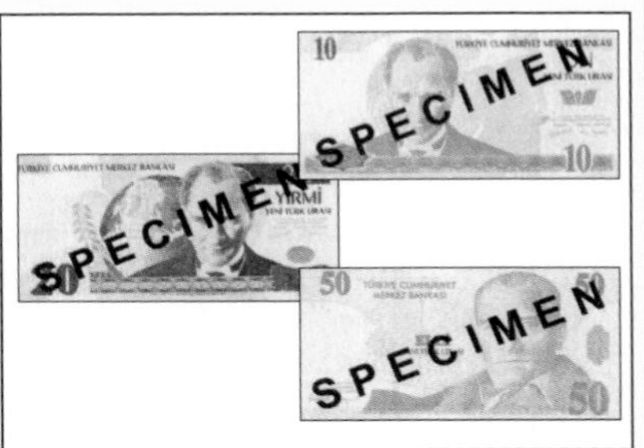

TIME

Turkey is two hours ahead of GMT, and operates a summertime from late March to late October when clocks are put forward one hour.

CUSTOMS

YES

Goods Obtained Duty Free taken into Turkey
(Limits):
Wine or spirits: 5l
Cigarettes: 200
Cigars: 50
Chocolate: 1kg; sweets: 1kg
Coffee:1.5kg
Instant coffee: 1.5kg instant
Tea: 500gm
Tobacco: 200gm
Perfume: 5 bottles (each 120ml max)
Toilet water: no limit

Airports have duty free facilities at entry points; some are open 24 hours.

No more than US$5,000-worth of Turkish YTL may be exported.

NO

Drugs, firearms, ammunition, offensive weapons, obscene material, unlicensed animals. The smuggling of drugs and antiquities both carry very severe penalties. If buying antiques or carpets (over 100 years old), get a clearance certificate from a museum before leaving the country.

HONORARY CONSULATES AND CONSULATES

UK
0242 244 5313

Germany
0242 322 9466

USA
0212 251 3602

Netherlands
0232 463 4960

Spain
0242 241 7770

WHEN YOU ARE THERE

TOURIST OFFICES

- Adana
  Çinarlı Mah, Atatürk Cad 13
  ☎ 0322 363 1448
- Alanya
  Damlataş Mağarası Yanı, Damlataş Cad 1
  ☎ 0242 513 1240
- Anamur
  Otogar Binası Kat 2
  ☎ 0324 814 3529
- Antalya
  Yavuz Özcan Parkı, (foot of Güllük Caddesi)
  ☎ 0242 241 1747
- Cappadocia
  Atatürk Bulv, Devlet Hastanesi Önü, Nevşehir
  ☎ 0384 212 9573
- Fethiye
  İskele Karşasi 1
  ☎ 0252 614 1527
- Kaş
  Cumhuriyet Meydanı 5
  ☎ 0242 836 1238
- Kemer
  Belediye ve Turizm Binası
  ☎ 0242 814 1537
- Marmaris
  İskele Meydanı 2
  ☎ 0252 313 0722
- Side
  Side Yoly Üzeri, Manavgat
  ☎ 0242 753 1265
- Silifke
  Gazi Mah, Veli Gürten Bozbey Cad 6
  ☎ 0324 714 1151

NATIONAL HOLIDAYS

J	F	M	A	M	J	J	A	S	O	N	D
1	(1)	1(3)	1				1		1		

1 Jan — New Year's Day
23 Apr — National Independence and Children's Day
19 May — Atatürk Commemoration and Youth and Sports Day
30 Aug — Victory Day
29 Oct — Republic Day

Moveable Holidays
Şeker Bayramı: Candy Festival to celebrate the end of the month-long Muslim fast of Ramazan.
Kurban Bayramı: Feast of the Sacrifice: meat is distributed to the poor. Both these holidays and Ramazan move backwards by 11 days each year. Ramazan began on 4 October in 2005 and begins on 23rd September in 2006.

OPENING HOURS

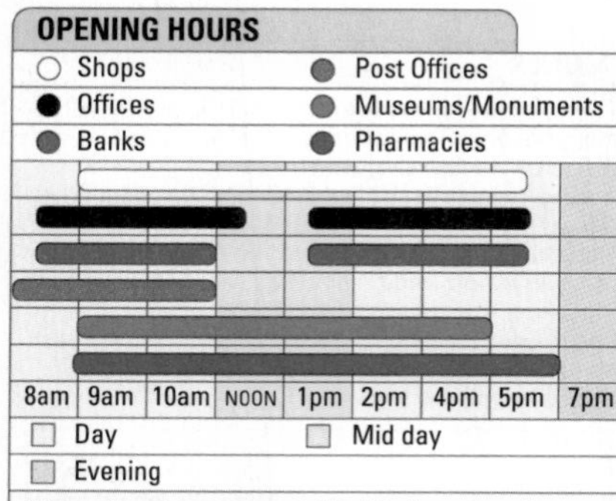

All opening times are variable. Markets open from Monday to Saturday (some on Sundays, too) 9–7. Major post offices open Monday to Saturday 8am–midnight and Sunday 9–7; minor post offices open during the week 8.30–12.30 and 1.30–5.30. Many archaeological sites have open access; those with formal opening hours tend to open daily 9–5. Many fuel stations open 24 hours, seven days a week. Banking hours are Mon–Fri 9–12, 1–5. Most have ATMs open 24 hours. Shops and pharmacies close on Sundays; museums on Mondays.

DRIVE ON THE
RIGHT

TOILETS
CHARGE

PUBLIC TRANSPORT

Internal Flights Domestic flights connect with most of the major regional centres.

Trains Due to the Toros Mountain range, trains do not run to any south coast cities other than Adana, Mersin and Tarsus. Intercity coaches operate between the main bus stations of each town. Several companies may operate on the same route and do not have integrated pricing or timetables.

Buses Buses are the most popular and practical means of getting around. The service is usually very reliable and professional. Tickets can be purchased at the bus station (*otogar*) in advance, and sometimes on the actual bus if you board after the starting point. Smoking is not allowed on buses.

Boat Trips Turkish Maritime Lines operate ferries between Fethiye and Ródos (Rhodes); from Alanya and Taşucu to Girne (Kyrenia) and from Mersin to Mağosa (Famagusta) in Turkish Cyprus (May to October).

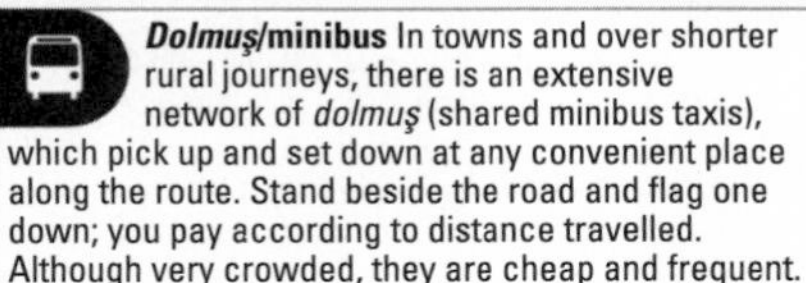

***Dolmuş*/minibus** In towns and over shorter rural journeys, there is an extensive network of *dolmuş* (shared minibus taxis), which pick up and set down at any convenient place along the route. Stand beside the road and flag one down; you pay according to distance travelled. Although very crowded, they are cheap and frequent.

CAR RENTAL

International car rental companies are all widely represented, with offices in the airports and at major towns and resorts. There are also many local firms. Advance booking is essential at peak periods and usually cost effective.

TAXIS

Yellow taxis are to be found on almost every street corner of every town. If the roof light is on, they are available for hire. Hotels and restaurants will call a cab if there is no convenient rank. All taxis have meters and reasonable, set tariffs.

DRIVING

Speed limit on motorways (*otoyol*): **120 kph (74.4mph)**

Speed limit on open roads: **90 kph (55.8mph)** for cars

Speed limit in urban areas: **50 kph (31mph)**

Seat belts must be worn in the front seat and in the rear if they are fitted.

There is a total ban on alcohol when driving.

Fuel is available as Super, Normal, and Unleaded (*kurşunsuz*) and Diesel. 24-hr fuel stations are plentiful on all major roads with full service, hygienic toilets and some have shops and cafés. Fuel prices are extremely high.

It is the policy of some of the British motoring organizations to include reciprocal arrangements with the TTOK—Turkish Touring and Automobile Club ☎ 0212 282 8140; www.turing.org.tr
If the car is hired, follow the instructions given in the documentation. It is imperative that all accidents are reported to the police. You must not move your vehicle until they arrive.

0 1 2 3 4 5 6 7 8
CENTIMETRES

INCHES
0 1 2 3

PERSONAL SAFETY

Turkey has a lower crime rate than may countries, but is now facing a dramatic rise in petty crime, particularly bag snatching. Women can expect plenty of flirting, but little real hassle. If you do feel threatened, appeal to the crowd. In towns, there are security police, traffic police and, in major resorts, tourist police who speak some foreign languages. In rural areas, policing is handled by the paramilitary *jandarma*. As anywhere, don't get enticed into lonely places.

Police assistance:
☎ 155
from any call box

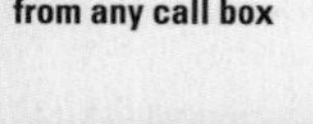

TELEPHONES

There are pay-phones on many streets, and at PTT offices. Phonecards are sold at post offices and newsagents. Most phones also accept credit cards. Main European mobile phones can be used here; North American visitors will need tri-band. Internet cafés are everywhere.

International Dialling Codes	
From Turkey to:	
UK:	**00 44**
Germany:	**00 49**
USA & Canada:	**00 1**
Netherlands:	**00 31**
Spain:	**00 34**

POST

Post offices (*postane*) are recognisable by their large yellow signs with PTT written in black. All major post offices operate *poste restante*, have foreign exchange desks and have public phones. Stamps are available from post offices, and from some sweet and souvenir shops and hotels.

ELECTRICITY

220V AC. Sockets accept standard continental two-pin plugs. Visitors from the UK require a 13-pin adaptor and US visitors will need a voltage transformer. Power cuts are frequent but usually short-lived in rural areas.

TIPS/GRATUITIES

Yes ✓ No ✗

Restaurants (service included)	✓	10%
Cafés/Bar (service not inc.)	✓	10%
Taxis	✓	round up
Tour guides	✓	10–15%
Porters	✓	1.5–2 YTL
Chambermaids	✓	1.5–2 YTL
Toilets	✓	50 kuruş
Masseurs/masseuses	✓	10%
Shoe attendants in mosques	✓	10%

What to photograph: everything. Turkey is immensely photogenic.
What not to photograph: always ask permission before photographing people. Strict Muslims may refuse, but many are delighted. Do not take photos of any military or police personnel or structure.
When to photograph: the midday sun is strong, the light flat and the shadows harsh. The best light for photography is in the early mornings and late afternoon.
Where to buy film: larger towns have photographic shops.

HEALTH

Insurance
All travellers are strongly advised to take out comprehensive travel insurance with good medical cover. There are some reciprocal health agreements, but generally you will pay first and are reimbursed later. Be sure you are specifically covered if you are planning to do any adventure sports.

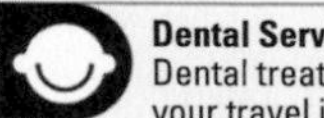

Dental Services
Dental treatment must be paid for. Check your travel insurance to see whether, and to what extent, dental treatment is covered.

Sun Advice
Avoid the midday sun: sunbathing should be rationed to prevent sunburn, heatstroke and longer-term skin damage. Use a high-factor sunblock.

Drugs
Pharmacies (*ezcane*) are plentiful and are a good first stop for treatment. Pharmacists routinely diagnose and treat minor conditions, while many drugs, including antibiotics that are only sold with a prescription in western Europe or the US are available over the counter. Hotels, tourist boards, tour operators' reps, consulates and pharmacists can recommend a good English-speaking doctor or state clinic. The private hospitals are generally good, clean and efficient.

Food and Water
The most likely ailment is simple diarrhoea, brought on by mild food poisoning, heatstroke or alcohol abuse (or a combination of all three). Avoid tap water: bottled mineral water is widely available. Avoid food that has been standing around in the open for any length of time.

CONCESSIONS

Most sights offer discounts for children.
There are some concessions on entrances to students with an International Student Identity Card (ISIC), and passengers with disabilities get a substantial discount on the trains. In general, however, the discounts are few and far between and apply only to native Turks.

CLOTHING SIZES

Turkey	UK	Rest of Europe		
46	36	46	36	Suits
48	38	48	38	
50	40	50	40	
52	42	52	42	
54	44	54	44	
56	46	56	46	
41	7	41	8	Shoes
42	7.5	42	8.5	
43	8.5	43	9.5	
44	9.5	44	10.5	
45	10.5	45	11.5	
46	11	46	12	
37	14.5	37	14.5	Shirts
38	15	38	15	
39/40	15.5	39/40	15.5	
41	16	41	16	
42	16.5	42	16.5	
43	17	43	17	
36	8	34	6	Dresses
38	10	36	8	
40	12	38	10	
42	14	40	12	
44	16	42	14	
46	18	44	16	
38	4.5	38	6	Shoes
38	5	38	6.5	
39	5.5	39	7	
39	6	39	7.5	
40	6.5	40	8	
41	7	41	8.5	

WHEN DEPARTING

- Reconfirm your flight 72 hours before you leave.
- Contact the airline/airport on the day before departure to ensure that flight details are unchanged.
- Keep exchange receipts, sales slips and VAT vouchers in your hand luggage if you wish to re-exchange money or claim tax back on any purchases.

LANGUAGE

Turkish, loosely related to Finnish and Hungarian, is an extremely difficult language that builds sentences by adding suffixes to the basic word, and keeps the verb at the end. The addition of a suffix can also alter the structure of the basic word and make it virtually unrecognisable to the untrained eye. Use a phrasebook and keep it simple. Pronunciation *ai/ay* long i, eg side; *c* a hard j, eg jam; *ç* ch, eg chat; *ı* er/uh, eg letter; *ğ* y; *ü* ew, eg few (roughly); *ö* ur (more like the Scandinanvian ø); *j* zh (no English equivalent); *ş* sh, eg shut.

hotel	*hotel/otel*	with a sea view	*deniz manzaralı*
bed and breakfast	*pansiyon*	balcony	*balkon*
do you have a room?	*boş odanız var mi?*	lift	*asansör*
single/double/triple	*tek/çift/üç kişilik*	room service	*oda servisi*
I have a reservation	*reservasyonım var*	air conditioning	*klima*
		central heating	*kalorifer*
		hot water	*sicak su*
		bath	*banyo*

bank	*banka*	expensive	*pahalı*
exchange office	*döriz*	what is the price?	*fıatı nedir?*
post office	*postane*	ten	*on*
travellers' cheque	*seyahat çeki*	fifty	*elli*
credit card	*kredi kartı*	one hundred	*yüz*
exchange rate	*dövis kuru*	two hundred	*ikiyüz*
how much?	*ne kadar?*	one thousand	*bin*

I'd like a table for two	*iki kişilik bir masa*	vegetarian dishes	*etsiz yemekler*
waiter	*garson*	bread	*ekmek*
menu	*fiyat listesi*	beer	*bira*
soup	*çorba*	red/white wine	*kırmızı/beyaz şarap*
fish	*balık*		
meat dishes	*etli yemekler*	bill	*hesap*
fruit	*meyva*	service included	*servos dahilli*

aeroplane	*uçak*	car	*araba*
airport	*havaalanı*	petrol	*benzin (super/normal)*
train	*tren*		
railway station	*tren ıstasyonu*	boat	*gemi*
bus	*otobus*	ferry	*vapur/feribot*
bus stop	*emanet*	port/harbour	*liman*
bus station	*otogar*	ticket	*bilet*
taxi	*taksi*	single/return	*gidiş/gidiş dönüş*

hello	*merhaba*	you're welcome	*bir şey değil*
goodbye	*allaha ısmarladık (person going)*	I don't understand	*sizi anlamiyorum*
goodbye	*güle güle (person staying)*	do you speak English?	*İngilizce biliyor musunuz?*
yes	*evet*		
no	*hayır/yok*		
please	*lütfen*	open	*açik*
thank you	*teşekkür ederim/mersi*	closed	*kapalı*
		leave me alone	*bırak beni*

INDEX

Acknowledgements
The Automobile Association wishes to thank the following photographers and libraries for their assistance in the preparation of this book.
AKG LONDON 10b (Erich Lessing);; ART DIRECTORS/ TRIP PHOTO LIBRARY 90b (M Jenkin); ROBERT HARDING PICTURE LIBRARY 46, 47, 63; PICTURES COLOUR LIBRARY 92; M SHALES 40b, 41, 61, 91b; SPECTRUM COLOUR LIBRARY 23b; WORLD PICTURES 62. All remaining pictures are held in the Association's own library (AA PHOTO LIBRARY) and were taken by Jean François Pin with exception of the following: P Bennett F/cover (a) fish meal, (b) ice-cream seller, (h) lemons, B/cover rafting, 12b, 37, 78b, 79, 129; P Kenward F/cover (c) paraglider, (d) painted doll, (e) Didyma temple, 8c, 13a, 15a, 16a, 16b, 17a, 18a, 18b, 19a, 20a, 21a, 22a, 23a, 24a, 24b, 24/5, 25a, 25b, 26a, 26b, 28/9, 31b, 32b, 32/3, 34a, 34b, 35b, 43a, 44, 49, 51b, 52, 53a, 54a, 54b, 56a, 57a, 58a, 60a, 64a, 65a, 65b, 66/7, 68a, 70a, 71b, 72, 74, 76b, 77, 81, 84, 89, 117a; D Mitideri 2, 9c, 27b, 42, 51a, 68c, 69, 88; T Souter 50

Author's Acknowledgements
The author would like to thank the following people and organisations for their generous assistance during the researching of this book: Dwynwen Berry, for driving long hours on perilous roads; Wanda Etheridge in Tarsus, Brigitta Dikmen in Kemer, and Mustafa Aydın and Ferhat Malcan in Kaş for invaluable information; Peter Espley of the Turkish Tourist Office in London; Sarah Moy of the Marketing Machine, Sunquest Holidays, Sheraton Hotels, the Hotel Club Green Fugla Beach, Inçekum, and the Sultan Saray Hotel, Kemer for assistance with accommodation.

Original edition copy editor: Nia Williams
Revision management: Apostrophe S Limited

Page Layout: Design 23

Dear Essential Traveller

Your comments, opinions and recommendations are very important to us. So please help us to improve our travel guides by taking a few minutes to complete this simple questionnaire.

You do not need a stamp (unless posted outside the UK). If you do not want to cut this page from your guide, then photocopy it or write your answers on a plain sheet of paper.

Send to: **The Editor, AA World Travel Guides, FREEPOST SCE 4598, Basingstoke RG21 4GY.**

Your recommendations...

We always encourage readers' recommendations for restaurants, nightlife or shopping – if your recommendation is used in the next edition of the guide, we will send you a ***FREE*** **AA *Essential* Guide** of your choice. Please state below the establishment name, location and your reasons for recommending it.

____

____

____

____

Please send me **AA *Essential*** ________________________

About this guide...

Which title did you buy?
AA *Essential* ________________________
Where did you buy it?________________________
When? m m / y y

Why did you choose an AA *Essential* Guide?____________________

____

____

____

____

Did this guide meet your expectations?
Exceeded ☐ Met all ☐ Met most ☐ Fell below ☐
Please give your reasons________________________

____

____

____

continued on next page...

Were there any aspects of this guide that you particularly liked? ___________

____

____

Is there anything we could have done better? ___________________

____

____

About you...

Name (*Mr/Mrs/Ms*) _______________________________

Address _______________________________________

____

_______________________ Postcode _______________

Daytime tel nos ________________________________

Please only give us your mobile phone number if you wish to hear from us about other products and services from the AA and partners by text or mms.

Which age group are you in?

Under 25 ☐ 25–34 ☐ 35–44 ☐ 45–54 ☐ 55–64 ☐ 65+ ☐

How many trips do you make a year?

Less than one ☐ One ☐ Two ☐ Three or more ☐

Are you an AA member? Yes ☐ No ☐

About your trip...

When did you book? m m / y y When did you travel? m m / y y

How long did you stay? ____________________________

Was it for business or leisure? _______________________

Did you buy any other travel guides for your trip?

If yes, which ones? ____________________________

Thank you for taking the time to complete this questionnaire. Please send it to us as soon as possible, and remember, you do not need a stamp (*unless posted outside the UK*).

Happy Holidays!

The information we hold about you will be used to provide the products and services requested and for identification, account administration, analysis, and fraud/loss prevention purposes. More details about how that information is used is in our privacy statement, which you'll find under the heading "Personal Information" in our terms and conditions and on our website: www.theAA.com. Copies are also available from us by post, by contacting the Data Protection Manager at AA, Southwood East, Apollo Rise, Farnborough, Hampshire GU14 OJW.

We may want to contact you about other products and services provided by us, or our partners (by mail, telephone) but please tick the box if you DO NOT wish to hear about such products and services from us by mail or telephone. ☐

The Atlas

Paul Kenward: *The chic new marina in Antalya which has been converted from the old harbour*

www.theAA.com
The Automobile Association's website offers comprehensive and up-to-the-minute information covering AA-approved hotels, guest houses and B&Bs, restaurants and pubs in the UK; airport parking, insurance, European breakdown cover, European motoring advice, a ferry planner, European route planner, overseas fuel prices, a bookshop and much more.

The Foreign and Commonwealth Office
Country advice, traveller's tips, before you go information, checklists and more.
www.fco.gov.uk

Official Tourist Information in UK
www.tourismturkey.gov

Official Tourist Information in US
www.turizm.tr

GENERAL
UK Passport Service
www.ukpa.gov.uk

Health Advice for Travelers
www.doh.gov.uk/traveladvice

BBC—Holiday
www.bbc.co.uk/holiday

The Full Universal Currency Coverter
www.xe.com/ucc/full.shtml

Flying with Kids
www.flying with kids

TRAVEL
Flights and Information
www.cheapflights.co.uk
www.thisistravel.co.uk
www.ba.com
www.worldairportguide.com

Turkish Touring and Automobile Club
www.turing.org.tr

le Mans-Est 4 — Motorway with junction

Date, Datum — Motorway under construction
Autobahn in Bau

Date, Datum — Motorway projected
Autobahn in Planung

Roadside restaurant and hotel
Raststätte mit Übernachtungsmöglichkeit

Roadside restaurant
Raststätte ohne Übernachtungsmöglichkeit

Snack bar, kiosk
Erfrischungsstelle, Kiosk

Filling station, Truck stop
Tankstelle, Autohof

Dual carriageway with motorway characteristics with junction
Autobahnähnliche Schnellstraße mit Anschlussstelle

Dual carriageway
Straße mit zwei getrennten Fahrbahnen

Thoroughfare
Durchgangsstraße

Important main road
Wichtige Hauptstraße

Main road
Hauptstraße

Other road
Sonstige Straße

Main line railway
Fernverkehrsbahn

Mountain railway
Bergbahn

Car ferry
Autofähre

Route with beautiful scenery
Landschaftlich besonders schöne Strecke

Routes des Crêtes — Tourist route
Touristenstraße

Toll road
Straße gegen Gebühr befahrbar

Road closed to motor traffic
Straße für Kraftfahrzeuge gesperrt

Temporarily regulated traffic
Zeitlich geregelter Verkehr

15% — Important gradients
Bedeutende Steigungen

Culture
Kultur

★★ PARIS
★★ *la Alhambra*
Worth a journey
Eine Reise wert

★ TRENTO
★ *Comburg*
Worth a detour
Lohnt einen Umweg

Landscape
Landschaft

★★ Rodos
★★ *Fingal's cave*
Worth a journey
Eine Reise wert

★ Korab
★ *Jaskinia raj*
Worth a detour
Lohnt einen Umweg

Important panoramic view
Besonders schöner Ausblick

National park, nature park
Nationalpark, Naturpark

4807 — Mountain summit with height in metres
Bergspitze mit Höhenangabe in Metern

(630) — Elevation
Ortshöhe

Church
Kirche

Church ruin
Kirchenruine

Monastery
Kloster

Monastery ruin
Klosterruine

Palace, castle
Schloss, Burg

Palace ruin, castle ruin
Schloss-, Burgruine

Monument
Denkmal

Waterfall
Wasserfall

Cave
Höhle

Ruins
Ruinenstätte

Other object
Sonstiges Objekt

Youth hostel
Jugendherberge

Airport
Verkehrsflughafen

Regional airport · Airfield
Regionalflughafen · Flugplatz

0 — 20 — 40 km
0 — 10 — 20 miles

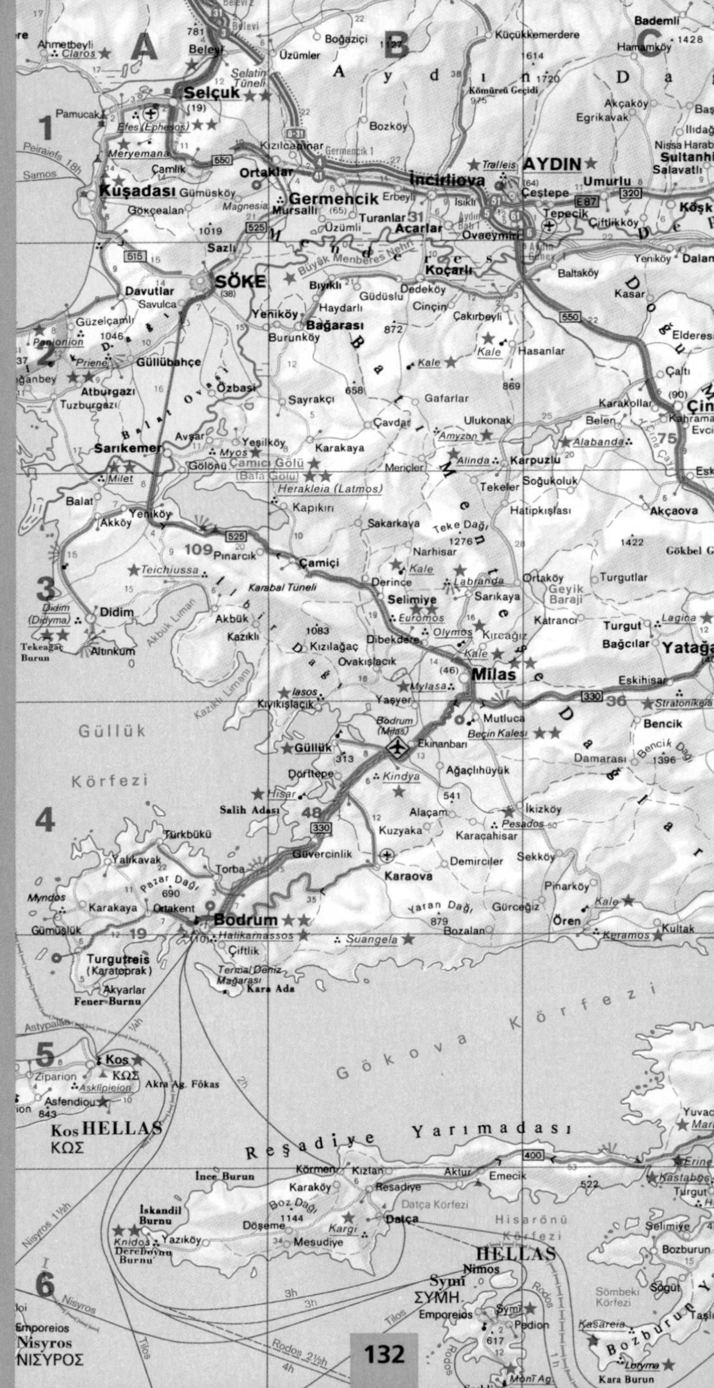

A
B
C
1
2
3
4
5
6
Ahmetbeyli
Claros
Belevi
Boğaziçi
Küçükkemerdere
Bademli
Hamamköy
Üzümler
Selatin Tüneli
Aydın Dağ
Kömürcü Geçidi
Selçuk
Pamucak
Efes (Ephesos)
Bozköy
Akçaköy
Egrikavak
Ilıdağ
Nissa Harabe
Sultanhisar
Salavatlı
Meryemana
Kızılcapınar
Germencik
Tralleis
AYDIN
Samos
Çamlık
Ortaklar
İncirliova
Umurlu
Kuşadası
Gümüşköy
Magnesia
Mursallı
Germencik
Erbeyli
Işıklı
Çeştepe
Köşk
Gökçealan
Turanlar
Üzümli
Acarlar
Ovaeymiri
Tepecik
Çiftlikköy
Sazlı
Büyük Menderes Nehri
Koçarlı
Yeniköy
Dalama
SÖKE
Bıyıklı
Güdüslu
Dedeköy
Baltaköy
Davutlar
Savulca
Haydarlı
Kasar
Güzelçamlı
Yeniköy
Bağarası
Burunköy
Cinçin
Çakırbeyli
Elderesi
Panionion
Kale
Hasanlar
Priene
Güllübahçe
Atburgazi
Tuzburgazi
Özbaşı
Sayrakçı
Gafarlar
Çaltı
Karakollar
Çine
Balat Ovası
Çavdar
Ulukonak
Belen
Kahraman
Evcil
Avşar
Yeşilköy
Amyzon
Alabanda
Sarıkemer
Myos
Karakaya
Alinda
Karpuzlu
Gölönü
Camıcı Gölü
(Bafa Gölü)
Mericler
Soğukoluk
Milet
Herakleia (Latmos)
Tekeler
Balat
Kapıkırı
Hatipkışlası
Akçaova
Akköy
Yeniköy
Sakarkaya
Teke Dağı
Pınarcık
Narhisar
Gökbel
Teichiussa
Çamiçi
Kale
Labranda
Ortaköy
Turgutlar
Karabal Tüneli
Derince
Geyik Barajı
Selimiye
Sarıkaya
Didim (Didyma)
Didim
Euromos
Katrancı
Turgut
Lagina
Akbük
Akbük Limanı
Olymos
Kırcağız
Bağcılar
Yatağan
Kazıklı
Kızılağaç
Dibekdere
Tekeağaç Burun
Altınkum
Ovakışlacık
Kale
Milas
Eskihisar
Iasos
Mylasa
Stratonikeia
Kıyıkışlacık
Yaşyer
Bodrum (Milas)
Mutluca
Bencik
Güllük
Kazıklı Limanı
Beçin Kalesi
Güllük
Ekinanbarı
Bencik Dağı
Damarası
Körfezi
Dörttepe
Ağaçlıhüyük
Kindya
Hisar
Salih Adası
Alaçam
İkizköy
Pesados
Kuzyaka
Karaçahisar
Türkbükü
Güvercinlik
Yalıkavak
Demirciler
Sekköy
Torba
Karaova
Pazar Dağı
Pınarköy
Myndos
Karakaya
Ortakent
Yaran Dağı
Gürceğiz
Kale
Bodrum
Ören
Gümüşlük
Halikarnassos
Suangela
Bozalan
Keramos
Kultak
Çiftlik
Turgutreis (Karatoprak)
Termal Deniz Mağarası
Kara Ada
Akyarlar
Fener Burnu
Gökova Körfezi
Astypalaia
Kos
ΚΩΣ
Ziparion
Asklipieion
Akra Ag. Fokas
Asfendiou
Kos HELLAS
ΚΩΣ
Reşadiye Yarımadası
Yuvacık
Marmaris
Körmen
Kızlan
Aktur
Emecik
Erine
Kastabos
İnce Burun
Karaköy
Reşadiye
Turgut
Boz Dağı
Datça Körfezi
Hisarönü Körfezi
İskandil Burnu
Döşeme
Kargi
Datça
Selimiye
Knidos
Yazıköy
Bozburun
Dereboynu Burnu
HELLAS
Nimos
Symi
ΣΥΜΗ
Sömbeki Körfezi
Söğüt
Emporeios
Symi
Pedion
Taşlıca
Kasareia
Emporeios
Nisyros
ΝΙΣΥΡΟΣ
Bozburun
Loryma
Kara Burun

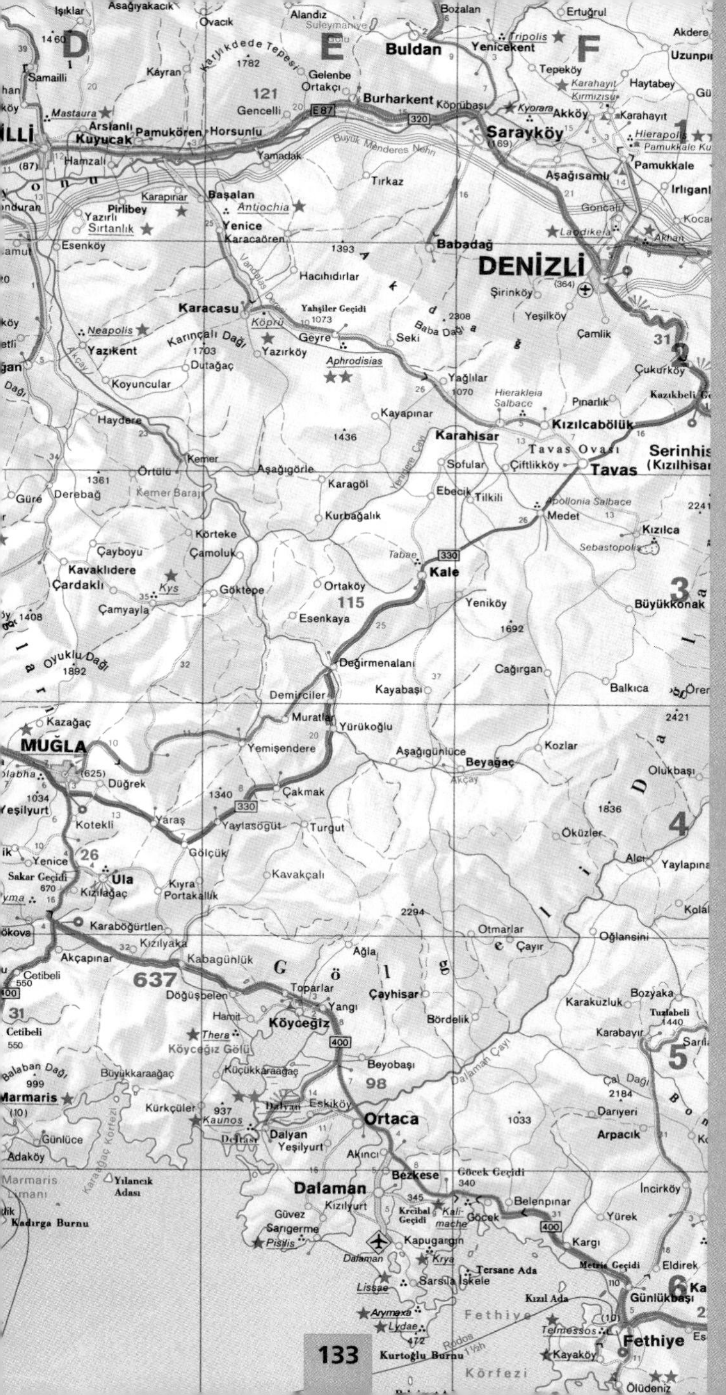
D
E
F
Işıklar
Asağıyakacık
Ovacık
Alandız
Suleymaniye Gölü
Bozalan
Ertuğrul
Akdere
Uzunpı
Buldan
Yenicekent
Tripolis
Karıkdede Tepesi
1782
Kayran
Gelenbe
Ortakçı
Samaili
Tepeköy
Karahayıt
Kırmızısu
Haytabey
121
Burharkent
Köprübaşı
Kyorara
Akköy
Karahayıt
Gencelli
E87
320
Mastaura
Arslanlı
Pamukören
Horsunlu
Kuyucak
Sarayköy
(169)
Hierapolis
Pamukkale
Büyük Menderes Nehri
Hamzali
(87)
Yamadak
Pamukkale
Tırkaz
Aşağısamlı
Irlıganlı
Karapınar
Başalan
Pirlibey
Antiochia
Goncalı
Yazırlı
Sırtanlık
Yenice
Karacaören
Laodikeia
Akhan
Esenköy
1393
Babadağ
DENİZLİ
(364)
Hacıhıdırlar
Şirinköy
Karacasu
Yahşiler Geçidi
1073
2308
Yeşilköy
Köprü
Baba Dağı
Neapolis
Geyre
Seki
Çamlık
Karınçalı Dağı
1703
Yazırköy
Yazıkent
Aphrodisias
Dutağaç
Çukurköy
Koyuncular
Yağlılar
1070
Hierakleia Salbace
Pınarlık
Kazıkbeli
Haydere
Kayapınar
Kızılcabölük
1436
Karahisar
Tavas Ovası
Serinhisar
(Kızılhisar)
Kemer
Sofular
Çiftlikköy
Tavas
Örtülü
Aşağıgörle
1361
Karagöl
Derebağ
Kemer Barajı
Ebecik
Tilkili
Güre
Apollonia Salbace
Medet
2241
Kurbağalık
Körteke
Kızılca
Sebastopolis
Çayboyu
Çamoluk
Tabae
330
Kavaklıdere
Kale
Çardaklı
Ortaköy
Kys
Göktepe
3
Yeniköy
115
Büyükkonak
Çamyayla
1408
Esenkaya
1692
Oyuklu Dağı
1892
Değirmenalanı
Çağırgan
Kayabaşı
Balkıca
Ören
Demirciler
2421
Kazağaç
Muratlar
Yürükoğlu
MUĞLA
Yemişendere
Kozlar
(625)
Aşağıgünlüce
Beyağaç
Düğrek
Akçay
Olukbaşı
1034
1340
Çakmak
Yeşilyurt
1836
Kotekli
Yaraş
Yaylasöğüt
Turgut
4
Öküzler
26
Gölcük
Yenice
Alcı
Yaylapınar
Sakar Geçidi
670
Ula
Kavakçalı
Kıyra
Kızılağaç
Portakallık
Kolak
2294
Karaboğürtlen
Otmarlar
Oğlansini
Kızılyaka
Çayır
Akçapınar
Ağla
Kabagünlük
Çetibeli
550
637
Toparlar
Yangı
Çayhisar
Bozyaka
Döğüşbelen
Karakuzluk
31
Hamit
Köyceğiz
Bördelik
Tuzlabeli
1440
Thera
Karabayır
Köyceğiz Gölü
400
5
Balaban Dağı
999
Büyükkaraağaç
Küçükkaraağaç
Beyobaşı
Dalaman Çayı
98
Çal Dağı
2184
Marmaris
Kürkçüler
937
Dalyan
Eskiköy
Ortaca
Darıyeri
Kaunos
1033
Delrası
Dalyan
Arpacık
Günlüce
Yeşilyurt
Akıncı
Adaköy
Karaağaç Körfezi
Marmaris Limanı
Yılancık Adası
Bezkese
Göcek Geçidi
340
Dalaman
345
İncirköy
Belenpınar
Kadırga Burnu
Güvez
Kızılyurt
Kreibal Geçidi
Kalimache
Göcek
Yürek
Sarıgerme
Pisilis
Kapugargın
Kargı
Dalaman
Krya
Metris Geçidi
Eldirek
Tersane Ada
Lissae
Sarsıla İskele
6
Kızıl Ada
Günlükbaşı
Arymaxa
Fethiye
Lydae
Telmessos
472
Rodos
Fethiye
Kurtoğlu Burnu
Kayaköy
Körfezi
Ölüdeniz

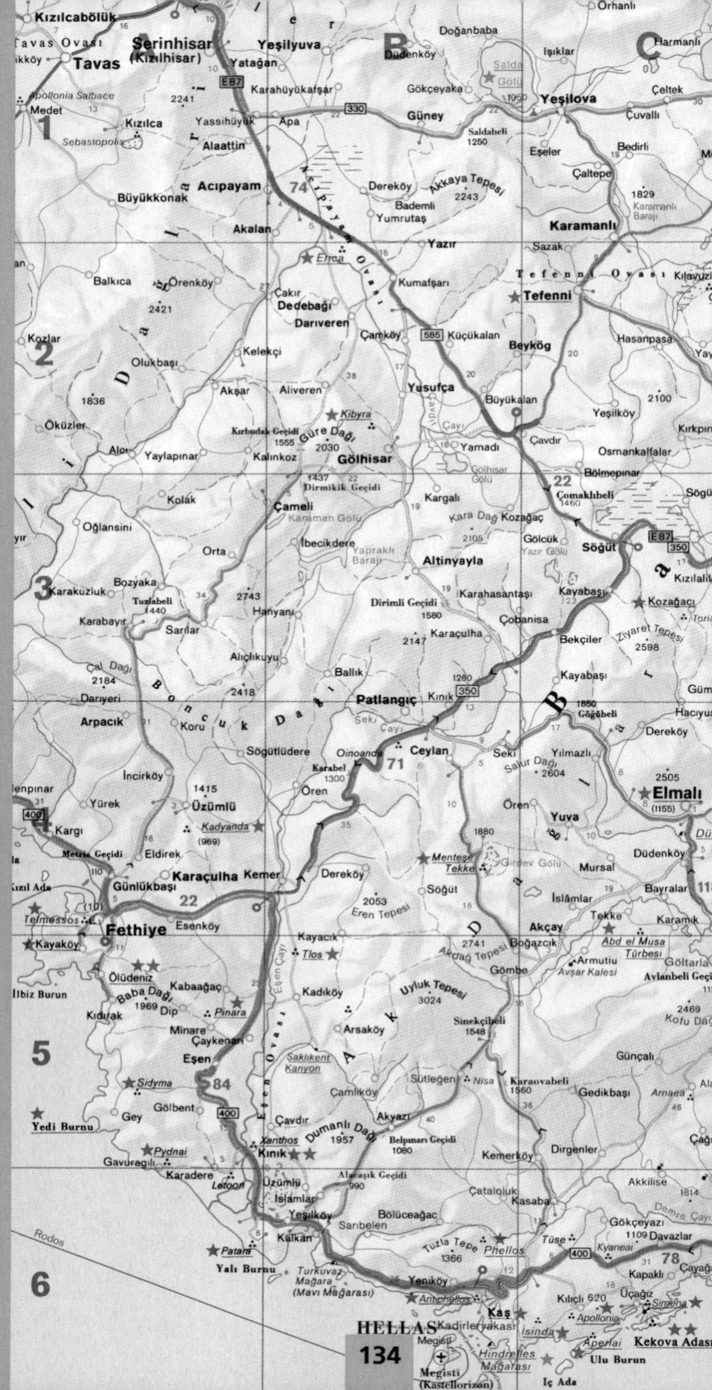

Kızılcabölük
Tavas Ovası
Tavas
Serinhisar (Kızılhisar)
Yeşilyuva
Yatağan
Düdenköy
Doğanbaba
Orhanlı
Harmanlı
Işıklar
Salda Gölü
Karahüyükafşar
Gökçeyaka
Yeşilova
Çeltek
Çuvallı
Apollonia Salbace
Medet
Kızılca
Sebastopolis
Yassıhüyük
Apa
Güney
Saldabeli 1250
Eşeler
Bedirli
Alaattin
Çaltepe
Acıpayam
Acıpayam Ovası
Dereköy
Akkaya Tepesi 2243
Bademli
Yumrutaş
Büyükkonak
Karamanlı
Karamanlı Barajı
Akalan
Yazır
Sazak
Eriza
Tefenni Ovası
Kılavuzlar
Balkıca
Örenköy
Kumafşarı
Tefenni
Çakır
Dedebağı
Darıveren
Çamköy
Küçükalan
Beyköğ
Hasanpaşa
Kozlar
Kelekçi
Olukbaşı
Akşar
Aliveren
Yusufça
Büyükalan
Yeşilköy
Dalaman Çayı
Kibyra
Öküzler
Kırbudak Geçidi 1555
Güre Dağı 2030
Yamadı
Çavdır
Kırkpınar
Alcı
Yaylapınar
Kalınkoz
Gölhisar
Gölhisar Gölü
Osmankalfalar
Bölmepınar
Dirmikik Geçidi
Kargalı
Çomaklıbeli 1460
Söğüt
Kolak
Çameli
Karaman Gölü
Kara Dağ
Kozağaç
Oğlansini
İbecikdere
Yapraklı Barajı
Gölcük
Yazır Gölü
Orta
Altınyayla
Kızılalil
Bozyaka
Karakuzluk
Tuzlabeli 1440
Dirimli Geçidi 1580
Karahasantaşı
Kayabaşı
Kozağacı
Karabayır
Sarılar
Hanyan
Çobanisa
Karaçulha
Bekçiler
Ziyaret Tepesi 2598
Çal Dağı 2184
Alıçlıkuyu
Ballık
Kayabaşı
Darıyeri
Boncuk Dağları
Patlangıç
Kınık
Arpacık
Koru
Seki Çayı
Göğübeli 1850
Hacıyus
Dereköy
Sögütlüdere
Oinoanda
Ceylan
Seki
Yılmazlı
Salur Dağı 2604
Karabel 1300
İncirköy
Yürek
Üzümlü
Ören
Ören
Yuva
Elmalı (1155)
Kargı
Kadyanda (969)
Metris Geçidi
Eldirek
Menteşe Tekke
Girdev Gölü
Mursal
Düdenköy
Kızıl Ada
Günlükbaşı
Karaçulha
Kemer
Dereköy
Söğüt
Bayralar
Eren Tepesi 2053
İslâmlar
Telmessos
Fethiye
Esenköy
Akçay
Tekke
Karamık
Kayaköy
Kayacık
Tlos
Akdağ Tepesi 2741
Boğazcık
Abd el Musa Türbesi
Armutlu
Avşar Kalesi
Göltarla
Ölüdeniz
Gömbe
Avlanbeli Geçidi
İlbiz Burun
Kabaağaç
Baba Dağı 1969
Kadıköy
Uyluk Tepesi 3024
Kıdırak
Dip
Pinara
Minare
Arsaköy
Sinekçibeli 1548
2469 Kofu Dağı
Çaykenarı
Eşen
Esen Çayı
Eşen Ovası
Saklıkent Kanyon
Güncalı
Sidyma
Sütleğen
Nisa
Karaovabeli 1560
Gedikbaşı
Arnaea
Yedi Burnu
Gey
Gölbent
Çamlıköy
Çavdır
Akyazı
Dumanlı Dağı 1957
Belpınarı Geçidi 1080
Dirgenler
Pydnai
Xanthos
Kınık
Kemerköy
Gavurağılı
Karadere
Letoon
Üzümlü
Alacaşık Geçidi 990
Akkilise
İslamlar
Çataloluk
Kasaba
Yeşilköy
Bölüceağac
Demre Çayı
Gökçeyazı
Rodos
Kalkan
Sarıbelen
Davazlar 1109
Patara
Tuzla Tepe 1366
Phellos
Tüse
Kyaneai
Kapaklı
Çayağzı
Yalı Burnu
Turkuvaz Mağara (Mavi Mağarası)
Yeniköy
Antiphellos
Kaş
Kılıçlı 620
Üçağız
Simena
Apollonia
HELLAS
134
Kadirleryakası
Megisti
İsinda
Aperlai
Kekova Adası
Hindirelles Mağarası
Megisti (Kastellorizon)
Ulu Burun
İç Ada

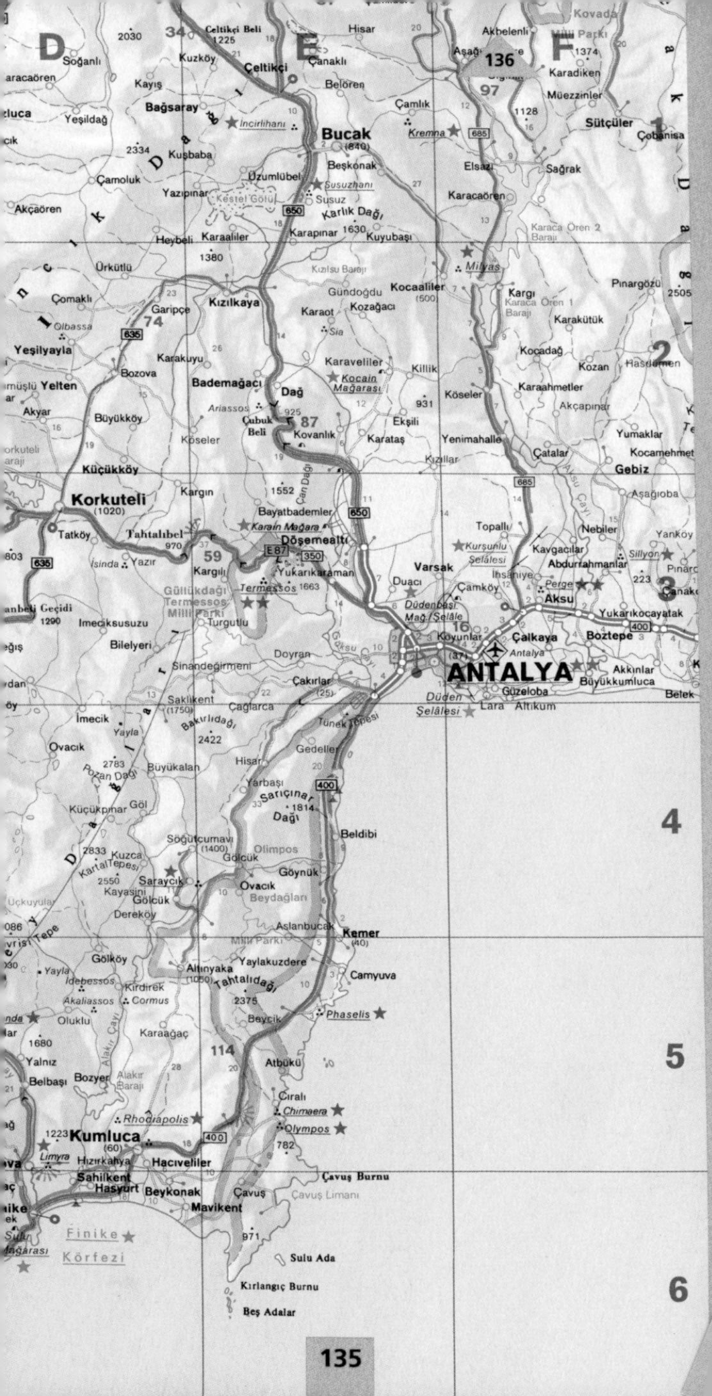

D
E
F
136
97
1
2
3
4
5
6
Bucak
Korkuteli
ANTALYA
Çeltikçi
Kemer
Kumluca
Beldibi
Göynük
Aksu
Varsak
Döşemealtı
Termessos
Phaselis
Olympos
Chimaera
Finike Körfezi
Çavuş Burnu
Sulu Ada
Kırlangıç Burnu
Beş Adalar

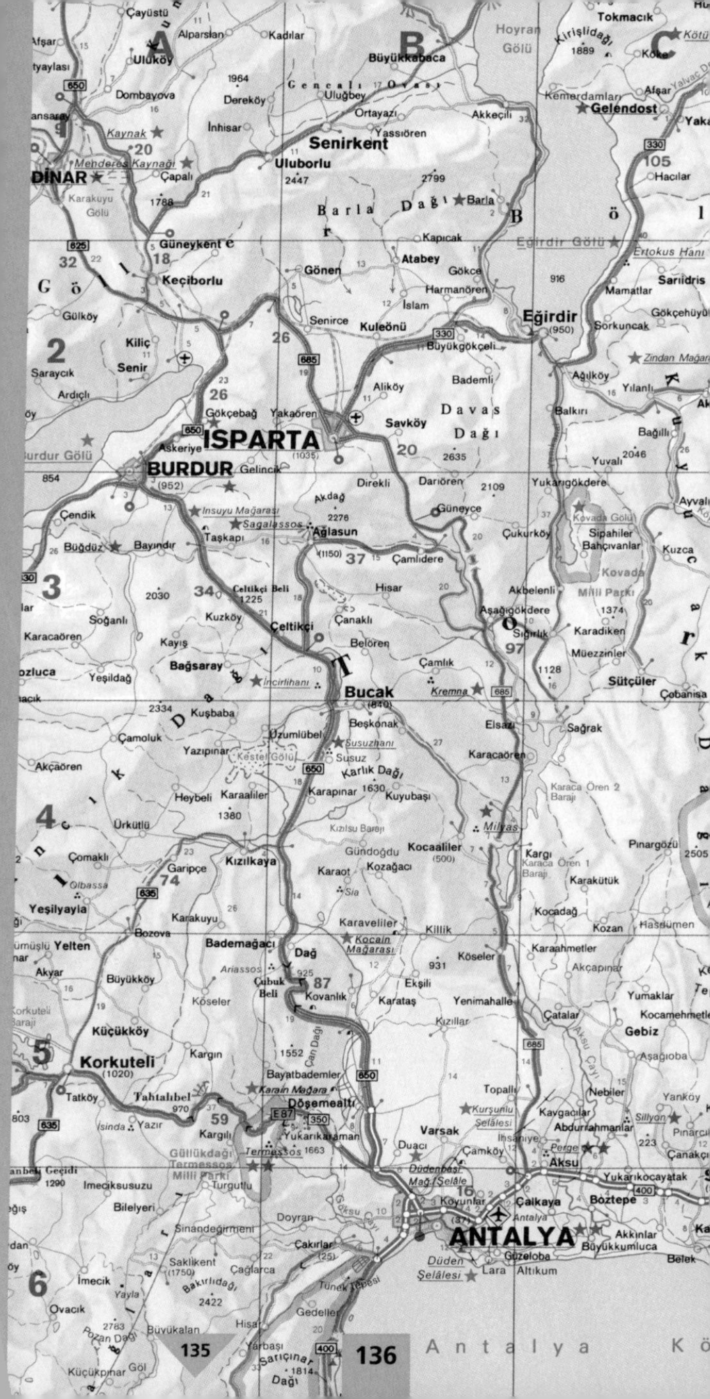

A
B
C
ISPARTA
BURDUR
ANTALYA
DİNAR
Eğirdir
Bucak
Korkuteli
Senirkent
Uluborlu
Keçiborlu
Gelendost
Ağlasun
Çeltikçi
Döşemealtı
Aksu
Burdur Gölü
Eğirdir Gölü
Barla Dağı
Davas Dağı
Antalya Körfezi

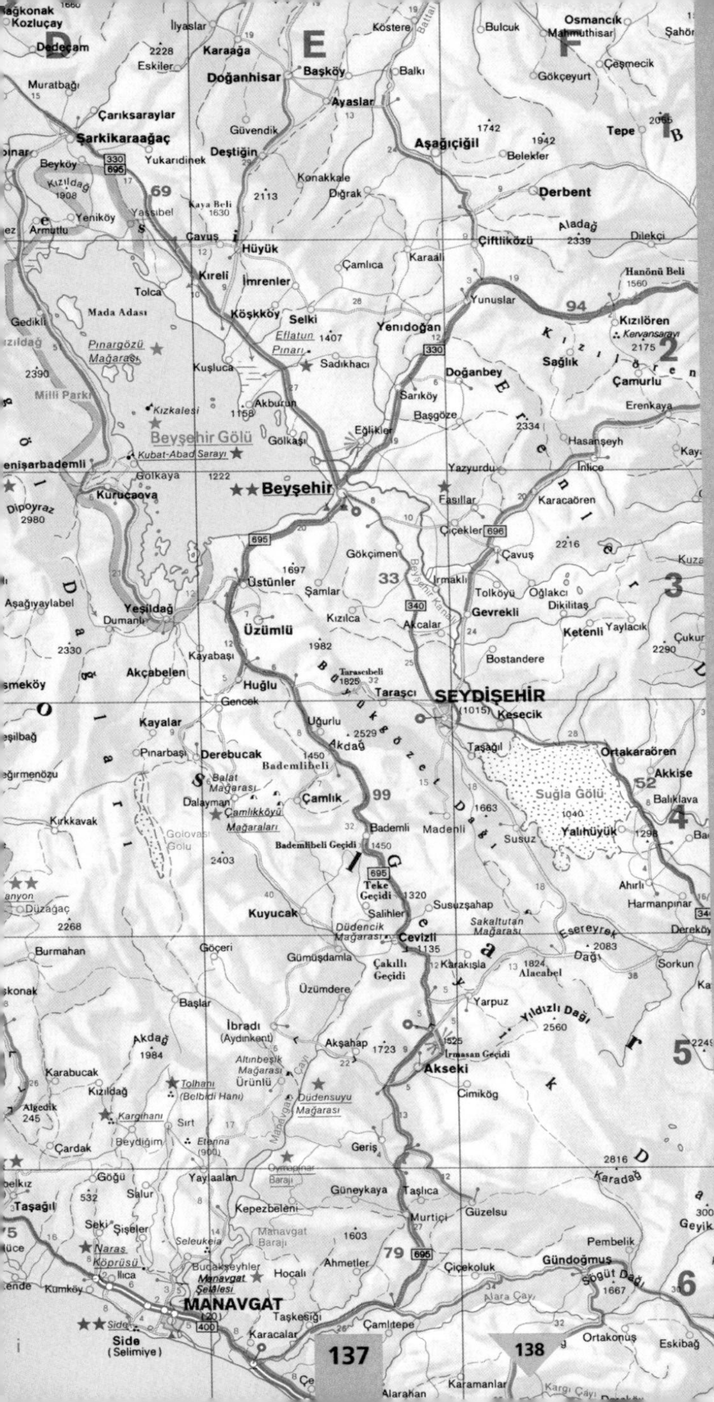
D
E
F
Kozluçay
Dedeçam
İlyaslar
Köstere
Bulcuk
Osmancık
Mahmuthisar
Şahör
Eskiler
Karaağa
Doğanhisar
Başköy
Balkı
Gökçeyurt
Çeşmecik
Muratbağı
Ayaslar
Çarıksaraylar
Güvendik
Tepe
Şarkikaraağaç
Deştiğin
Aşağıçiğil
Belekler
Beyköy
Yukarıdinek
Konakkale
Kızıldağ
Dığrak
Derbent
Kaya Beli
Yassıbel
Yeniköy
Armutlu
Aladağ
Çavuş
Hüyük
Çiftliközü
Dilekçi
Çamlıca
Karaali
Kıreli
İmrenler
Hanönü Beli
Tolca
Yunuslar
Mada Adası
Gedikli
Köşkköy
Selki
Yenıdoğan
Kızılören
Kervansarayı
Eflatun Pınarı
Pınargözü Mağarası
Sadıkhacı
Sağlık
Kuşluca
Doğanbey
Çamurlu
Milli Parkı
Sarıköy
Akburun
Erenkaya
Kızkalesi
Başgöze
Beyşehir Gölü
Gölkaşı
Eğlikler
Hasanşeyh
Kubat-Abad Sarayı
Yazyurdu
İnlice
Gölkaya
Beyşehir
Kurucaova
Fasıllar
Karacaören
Dipoyraz
Çiçekler
Gökçimen
Çavuş
Üstünler
Şamlar
Irmaklı
Beyşehir Kanalı
Tolköyü
Oğlakcı
Aşağıyaylabel
Yeşildağ
Dilikitaş
Dumanlı
Kızılca
Gevrekli
Üzümlü
Akcalar
Ketenli
Yaylacık
Kayabaşı
Bostandere
Akçabelen
Tarascıbeli
Huğlu
Tarașcı
Gencek
SEYDİŞEHİR
Kesecik
Kayalar
Uğurlu
Akdağ
Ortakaraören
Pınarbaşı
Derebucak
Taşağıl
Akkise
Bademlibeli
Balat Mağarası
Suğla Gölü
Dalayman
Çamlık
Balıklava
Çamlıkköyü Mağaraları
Kırkkavak
Golovası Golu
Bademli
Madenli
Susuz
Yalıhüyük
Bademlibeli Geçidi
Teke Geçidi
Ahırlı
Harmanpınar
Düzağaç
Kuyucak
Salihler
Susuzşahap
Sakaltutan Mağarası
Esereyrek Dağı
Dereköy
Düdencik Mağarası
Cevizli
Burmahan
Göçeri
Gümüşdamla
Çakıllı Geçidi
Karakışla
Alacabel
Sorkun
Üzümdere
Yarpuz
Başlar
İbradı (Aydınkent)
Yıldızlı Dağı
Akdağ
Akşahap
Irmasan Geçidi
Akseki
Karabucak
Altınbeşik Mağarası
Ürünlü
Tolhanı (Belbidi Hanı)
Kızıldağ
Düdensuyu Mağarası
Cimiköğ
Algedik
Kargıhanı
Sırt
Manavgat Çayı
Etenna
Çardak
Beydiğim
Geriş
Oymapınar Barajı
Göğü
Yaylaalan
Karadağ
Salur
Güneykaya
Taşlıca
Taşağıl
Kepezbeleni
Murtiçi
Güzelsu
Seki
Şişeler
Manavgat Barajı
Geyik
Seleukeia
Pembelik
Naras Köprüsü
Bucakşeyhler
Ahmetler
Çiçekoluk
Gündoğmuş
Söğüt Dağı
Ilıca
Manavgat Şelalesi
Hocalı
Kumköy
Alara Çayı
MANAVGAT
Taşkesiği
Side
Çamlıtepe
Ortakonuş
Eskibağ
Karacalar
Selimiye
Alarahan
Karamanlar
Kargı Çayı
138

A
B
C
137
1
2
3
4
5
6
Sütçüler
Çobanisa
Kesmeköy
Akçabelen
Yeşildağ
Üzümlü
Kayabaşı
Huğlu
Gencek
Kızılca
Taraşcı
Kayalar
Yeşilbağ
Pınarbaşı
Derebucak
Değirmenözu
Uğurlu
Akdağ
Bademlibeli
Balat Mağarası
Dalayman
Çamlık
Çamlıkköyü Mağaraları
Kırkkavak
Pınargözü
Ballıbucak
Çaltepe
Bademli
Bademlibeli Geçidi
Köprülü Kanyon
Altınkaya (Zerk)
Selge (950)
Düzağaç
Milli Parkı
Oluk Köprü
Teke Geçidi
Salihler
Kuyucak
Düdencik Mağarası
Cevizli
Kozan
Hasdümen
Burmahan
Göçeri
Gümüşdamla
Çakıllı Geçidi
Keriz Tepesi
Yumaklar
Karabük
Beşkonak
Üzümdere
Başlar
Kocamehmetler
Gebiz
İbradı (Aydınkent)
Akdağ
Akşahap
Aşağıoba
Altınbeşik Mağarası
Karabucak
Ürünlü
Nebiler
Bucak
Kızıldağ
Tolhanı (Belbidi Hanı)
Düdensuyu Mağarası
Yanköy
Kızıllar
Algedik
Sağırın
Sillyon
Pınarcık
Kargıhanı
Sırt
Çanakçı
Çardak
Beydiğim
Etenna (900)
Geriş
Aspendos
Oymapınar Barajı
Yukarıkocayatak
Serik (50)
Büyükbelkız (Belkıs)
Göğü
Yaylaalan
Güneykaya
Taşlıca
Boztepe
Taşağıl
Salur
Kepezbeleni
Murtiçi
Akkınlar
Karadayı
Seki
Şişeler
Manavgat Barajı
Büyükkumluca
Büklüce
Naras Köprüsü
Seleukeia
Ahmetler
Belek
Boğazak
Ilıca
Bucakşeyhler
Hocalı
Perakende
Kumköy
Manavgat Şelâlesi
MANAVGAT (20)
Taşkesiği
Side
Side (Selimiye)
Karacalar
Çamlıtepe
Antalya Körfezi
Çenger
Boztepe
Alarahan
Alara Han
Okurcalar
Incekum
400
695
340
Köprü Çayı
Manavgat Çayı

Çatören
May Barajı
Alibeyhüyüğü
Türkmencamili
Çukurçimen
Kayasu
Süleymanlı
Gökhüyük
İnli
Arıkören
Akören
Karahüyük
Köprü
Yenisu
Avdul
Yörükcamili
Ortakaraören
Akkise
Apasaraycık
Apa
Dineksaray
Balıklava
Apa Barajı
Yenimescit
Dinek
Aydoğmuş
Karasınır
Çiçekli
Bademli
Avdan
Beyşehir Kanalı
Afşar
Çiçekköy
Özyurt
Tahtalı
Güneysınır
Ahırlı
Aydınkışla
Kâzım Karabekir
Harmanpınar
Isauria
Vetus
Kuzören
Belören
Dereköy
Bozkır
Taşbaşı
Kızılçakır
Ağaçoba
Hisarlık
Yeniköy
Kayaağzı
Sorkun
Üçpınar
Kızılyaka
Kayapınar
Dereiçi
Hamzalar
Habiller
Alanözü
Bozkandak
Soğucak
Bağbaşı
Aşağıeşenler
Göçer
Göksu
Gaziler
Aladağ
Ağaççı
Dedemli
Hadım
Yerköprü Mağ.
Mağara Dağı
Yukarıkızılka
Korualan
Gevnebeli
Yukarıkızılkaya
Taşkent
Balcılar
Bayırköy
Karadağ
Afşar
Faşikan Geçidi
Çetmi
Balcılar
Geyik Dağı
Oyuklu Dağı
Pembelik
Beyreli
Çukuryurt
Çamiçi
Akdağ
Söğüt Dağı
Beden
Bağbelen
Akyar
Karahasan Geçidi
Basköy
Katranlı
Sulugöl Tepesi
Aşağıçağlar
Ortakonuş
Eskibağ
Köprülü
Sarıveliler
Üzümlü
Güneyyurt
Civandere
Adiller
Gevne Çayı
Ermenek
Dereköy
Civler
Tepebaşı
Küçük Çayı
Göktepe
Maraspoli Mağarası
Bademağacı
Şeyhler
Esentepe
Uğurlu
Öteköy
Çukurbağ
ALANYA
Alacami
Kızılaşehir
Gümüşkavak
Dumlugöze
Daran
Pınarönü
Ardıçkaya
Kale
Dim Çayı
Ermenek Çayı
Cebireis Dağı
Sapadere
Yunt Dağı
Kazancı
Çamyolu
Gözüküçüklü
Şeyhler
Mahmutlar
Syedra
Beldibi
Çamlıca
Sugözü
Taşeli
Belen
Kızıl Dağ
Ilıca
Demirtaş
Kızılgüney
Yaylası
İmamlı
Çörüş
Karaçal Tepesi
Sugözü
Çukurabanc
Kahyalar
Çığlık
Selinous
Karaçukur
Gazipaşa
Yenigüney
Akoluk
Hasdere
Doğanca
Yalan Dünya Mağarası
Işıklar
Anamur Çayı
Beyrebucak
Karaağa
Çamlıpınar
Akine
Girne (Keryneia) 3h
Kükür
Antiocheia ad Cragum
Göçük
Ovabaşı
Buğu Mağarası
Çarıklar
Uçarı
ANAMUR
Nasrettin
Mamure Kalesi
Anamurion
Anamuryum
Anamur Burnu

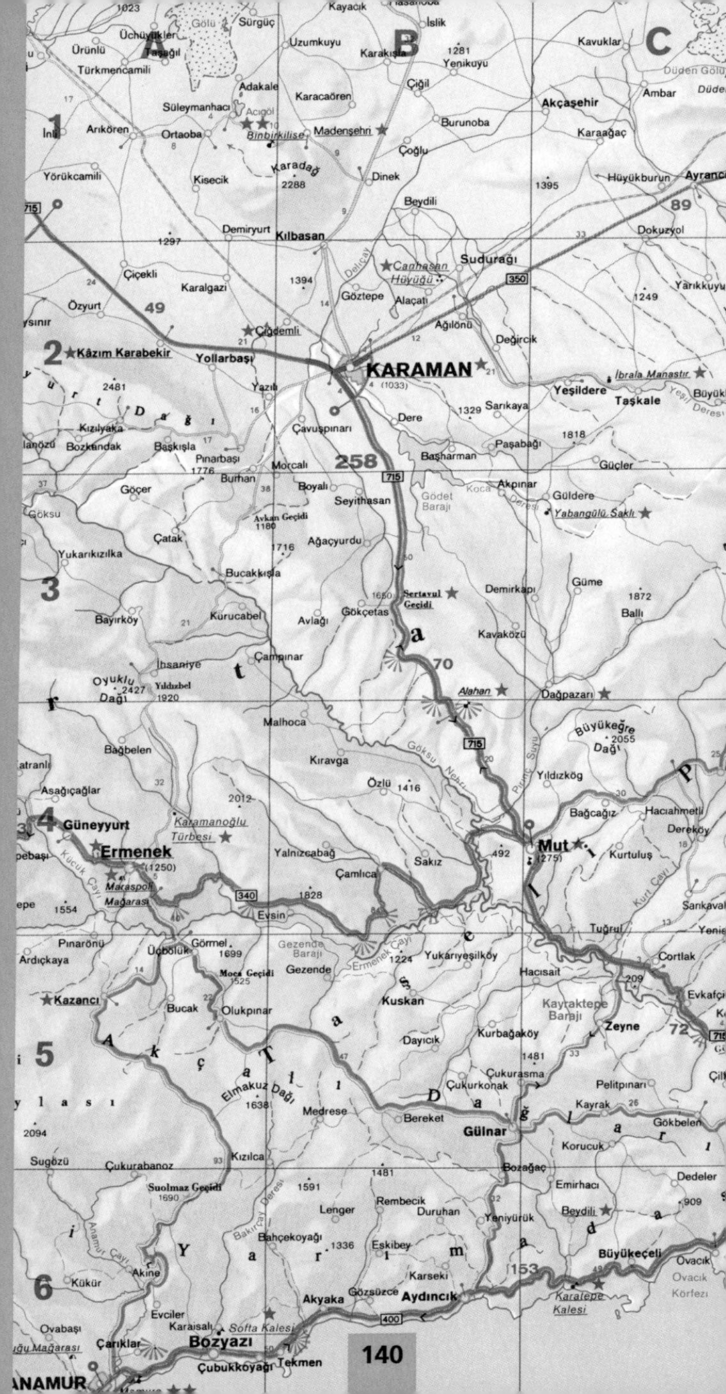

A
B
C
1
2
3
4
5
6
Kayacık
Sürgüç
İslik
Üchüyükler
Taşağıl
Ürünlü
Türkmencamili
Uzumkuyu
Karakışla
1281
Yenikuyu
Kavuklar
Düden Gölü
Adakale
Karacaören
Çiğil
Ambar
Süleymanhacı
Acıgöl
Binbirkilise
Madenşehri
Burunoba
Akçaşehir
Karaağaç
İnli
Arıkören
Ortaoba
Çoğlu
Karadağ
2288
Dinek
Yörükcamili
Kisecik
1395
Hüyükburun
Ayrancı
Beydili
89
715
Demiryurt
Kılbasan
1297
Dokuzyol
Çanhasan Hüyüğü
Sudurağı
Delıçay
Çiçekli
Karalgazi
1394
Göztepe
Alaçatı
350
Yarıkkuyu
1249
Özyurt
49
Ağılönü
Çiğdemli
Değircik
Kâzım Karabekir
Yollarbaşı
KARAMAN
(1033)
İbrala Manastır
Yeşildere
Taşkale
Büyükkoraş
2481
Yazılı
Dere
1329
Sarıkaya
Yeşil Dere
Kızılyaka
Çavuşpınarı
1818
Paşabağı
Bozkandak
Başkışla
Başharman
Pınarbaşı
1776
Burhan
Morcalı
258
Güçler
715
Göçer
Boyalı
Seyithasan
Gödet Barajı
Koca Deresi
Akpınar
Güldere
Yabangülü Saklı
Göksu
Avkan Geçidi
1180
Çatak
Ağaçyurdu
1716
Yukarıkızılka
Bucakkışla
Güme
Demirkapı
1872
Sertavul Geçidi
1650
Bayırköy
Kurucabel
Avlağı
Gökçetaş
Ballı
Kavaközü
İhsaniye
Çampınar
70
Oyuklu Dağı
2427
Yıldızbel
1920
Alahan
Dağpazarı
Malhoca
Büyükeğre Dağı
2055
Bağbelen
Kıravga
Göksu Nehri
Pirinç Suyu
Katranlı
Yıldızköğ
Özlü
1416
Bağcağız
Hacıahmetli
Aşağıçağlar
2012
Dereköy
Güneyyurt
Karamanoğlu Türbesi
Mut
(275)
Ermenek
Küçük Çayı
Yalnızcabağ
Sakız
492
Kurtuluş
(1250)
Maraspoli Mağarası
Çamlıca
Kurt Çayı
1554
340
1828
Sarıkavak
Evsin
Tuğrul
Pınarönü
Görmel
1699
Gezende Barajı
Ermenek Çayı
1224
Yukarıyeşilköy
Cortlak
Ardıçkaya
Üçbölük
Gezende
Hacısait
Moca Geçidi
1525
Kuskan
209
Evkafçiftliği
Kazancı
Bucak
Kayraktepe Barajı
Olukpınar
Zeyne
Kurbağaköy
72
Dayıcık
Elmakuz Dağı
1638
1481
Çukurasma
Çukurkonak
Pelitpınarı
2094
Medrese
Kayrak
Gökbelen
Bereket
Gülnar
Korucuk
Sugözü
Çukurabanoz
Kızılca
Bozağaç
Dedeler
Suolmaz Geçidi
1690
1591
Emirhacı
Lenger
Rembecik
Duruhan
Beydili
909
Bakırçay Deresi
Yeniyürük
Anamur Çayı
Bahçekoyağı
1336
Eskibey
Büyükeçeli
Ovacık
Akine
153
Ovacık Körfezi
Kükür
Karseki
Gözsüzce
Akyaka
Aydıncık
Karatepe Kalesi
Evciler
400
Ovabaşı
Karaisalı
Softa Kalesi
Çarıklar
Bozyazı
Çubukkoyağı
Tekmen
ANAMUR
Akdağlar
Taşeli
Yaylası
Akçatı Dağları
Yarım Dağı
Ermenek Çayı

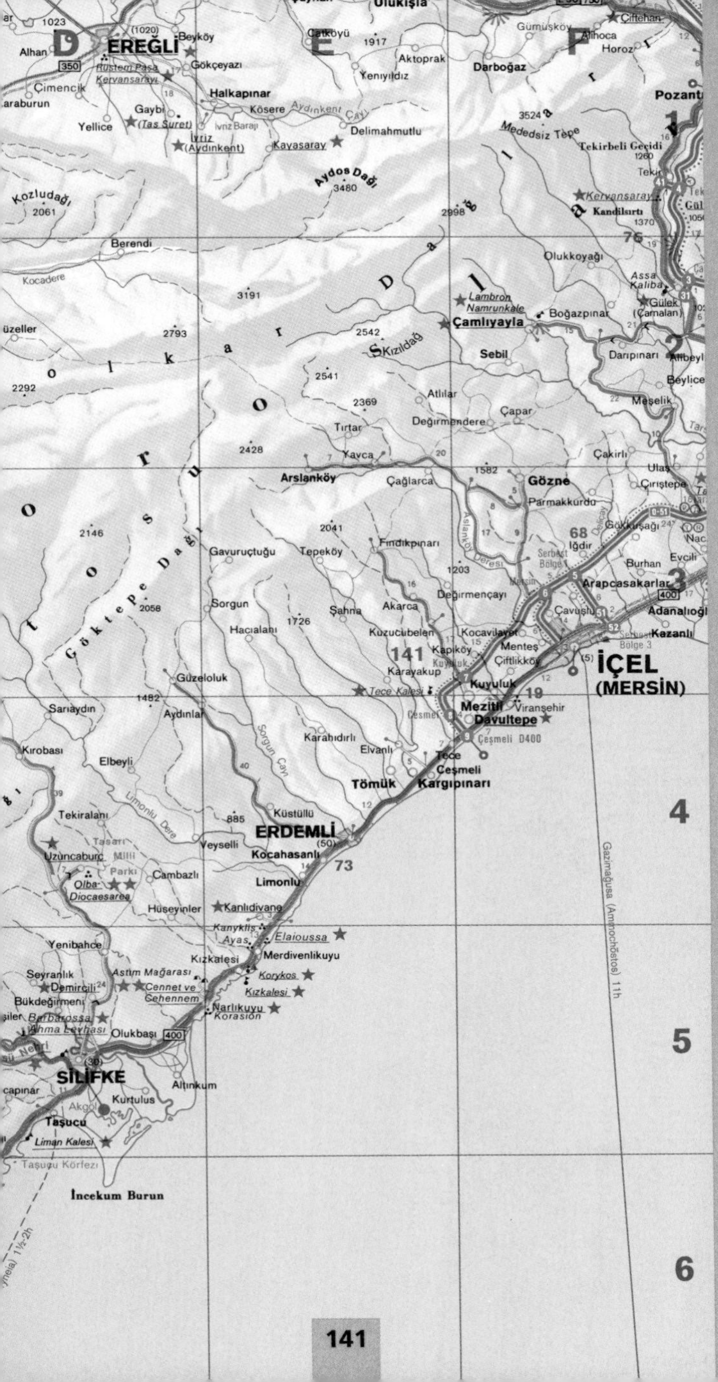

EREĞLİ
Rüstem Paşa Kervansarayı
Beyköy
Gökçeyazı
Halkapınar
Çimencik
Alhan
Gaybi
Yellice
Taş Suret
İvriz (Aydınkent)
Kösere
Delimahmutlu
Kayasaray
Çatköyü
Ulukışla
Aktoprak
Yeniyıldız
Darboğaz
Gümüşköy
Çiftehan
Alihoca
Horoz
Pozantı
Medetsiz Tepe
3524
Tekirbeli Geçidi
Kervansaray
Kandilsırtı
Aydos Dağı
3480
Kozludağı
2061
Berendi
Kocadere
3191
2793
2542
Kızıldağ
2541
2369
Olukkoyağı
Assa Kalıba
Gülek (Çamalan)
Lambron Namrunkale
Boğazpınar
Çamlıyayla
Sebil
Darıpınarı
Alibeyli
Beylice
Meşelik
Atlılar
Çapar
Değirmendere
Tırtar
Yavca
2428
2292
Arslanköy
Çağlarca
1582
Gözne
Parmakkurdu
Çakirli
Ulaş
Çırıştepe
Gökkuşağı
68
Iğdır
Serbest Bölge
Burhan
Evcili
Arapcasakarlar
Adanalıoğlu
Kazanlı
Çavuşlu
Serbest Bölge 3
2146
2041
Fındıkpınarı
Tepeköy
Gavuruçtuğu
Sorgun
2058
Göktepe Dağı
1203
Değirmençayı
Akarca
Şahna
1726
Hacıalanı
Kuzucubelen
Kocavilayet
Menteş
Çiftlikköy
Kapıköy
141
Karayakup
Kuyuluk
İÇEL (MERSİN)
Güzeloluk
1482
Sarıaydın
Aydınlar
Tece Kalesi
Mezitli
Viranşehir
Davultepe
Çeşmeli D400
Karahıdırlı
Elvanlı
Tece
Çeşmeli
Kargıpınarı
Tömük
Kırobası
Elbeyli
Sorgun Çayı
Limonlu Dere
Tekiralanı
885
Küstüllü
ERDEMLİ
Veyselli
Kocahasanlı
73
Limonlu
Uzuncaburç
Tasarı Milli Parkı
Olba-Diocaesarea
Cambazlı
Hüseyinler
Kanlıdivane
Kanykliş
Ayas
Elaioussa
Yenibahçe
Kızkalesi
Merdivenlikuyu
Seyranlık
Demircili
Astım Mağarası
Cennet ve Cehennem
Korykos
Kızkalesi
Bükdeğirmeni
Narlıkuyu
Korasion
Barbarossa
Ahma Levhası
Olukbaşı
SİLİFKE
Altınkum
Kurtuluş
Akgöl
Taşucu
Liman Kalesi
Taşucu Körfezi
İncekum Burun
Gazimağusa (Ammochōstos) 11h
Toroslar
Bolkar Dağları
D
E
F
1
2
3
4
5
6

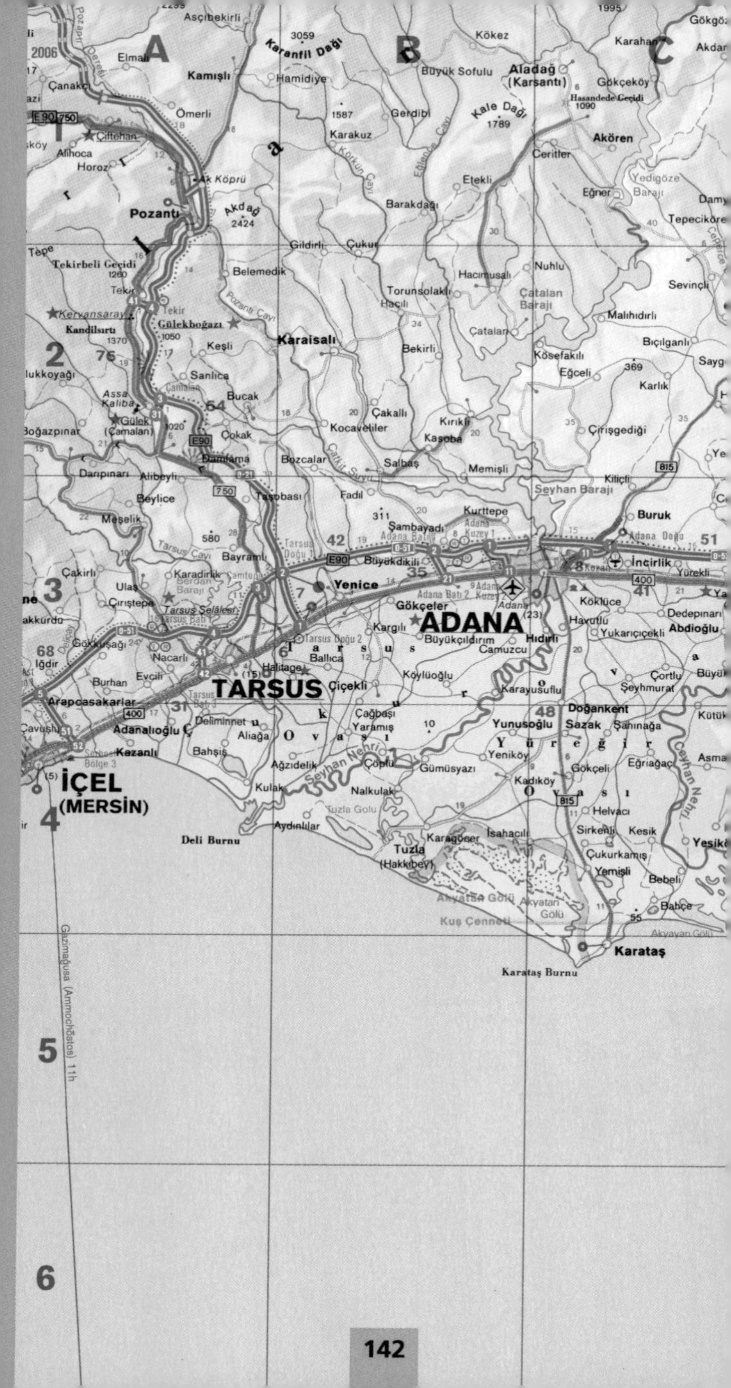

A
B
C
1
2
3
4
5
6
Pozantı
Karaisalı
Aladağ
(Karsantı)
Kamışlı
Çatalan Barajı
Seyhan Barajı
ADANA
TARSUS
İÇEL
(MERSİN)
İncirlik
Yenice
Karataş
Karataş Burnu
Deli Burnu
Tuzla
(Hakkıbey)
Akyatan Gölü
Kuş Cenneti
Seyhan Nehri
Ceyhan Nehri
Tekirbeli Geçidi
Gülekboğazı
Hasandede Geçidi
Karanfil Dağı
Kale Dağı
Akdağ
Gazimağusa (Ammochostos) 11h